THE ULTIMATE

Kids'

COOKBOOK

THE ULTIMATE

Kids'

COOKBOOK

Fun One-Pot Meals
Your Whole Family Will Love!

TIFFANY DAHLE

Founder of PEANUT BLOSSOM

PAGE STREET
PUBLISHING CO.

PAGE STREET
PUBLISHING CO.

First published in 2018 by
Page Street Publishing Co.
27 Congress Street, Suite 105
Salem, MA 01970
www.pagestreetpublishing.com

Distributed by Macmillan, sales in Canada by The Canadian Manda Group.

22   21   20   19   2   3   4   5

ISBN-13: 978-1-62414-583-4
ISBN-10: 1-62414-583-3

Library of Congress Control Number: 2018932233

Cover and book design by Page Street Publishing Co.
Photography by Tiffany Dahle

Printed and bound in China

For Sophie and Charlotte,
MY MOST PRECIOUS PEANUTS

TABLE OF CONTENTS

Introduction

DEAR FRIENDS, YOU'RE ABOUT TO COMPLETELY CHANGE YOUR DINNER ROUTINE FOR THE BETTER.

I am not a trained chef. I'm something way better: a real mom who understands the reality of feeding a crazy busy family. My two daughters love to cook in the kitchen with me, so we've tried just about every cookbook for kids you can find at the store. They always left us feeling disappointed. The food was either too simple or not delicious enough, or it took too much effort for too little result. Who has time to waste on failed recipes like that? Surely not me, and definitely not you.

Your lives are busy, and your schedule is packed. The kids would love to help cook, but you worry you don't have the time. It feels so much easier to just do it yourself and get it done.

Forcing yourself to do the cooking on your own doesn't sound like a lot of fun though, does it? What if making dinner together looked completely different? What if you got to end your day laughing and enjoying time with your family while the dinner gets made? Life is demanding, and we have to grab our opportunities to be together when we can and make our own joy.

The recipes you'll find here are simplified versions of classic recipes that I have streamlined for busy families. You'll discover many recipes that are a perfect fit for a hectic weeknight. And when life gets even too busy for that? I've got your weekends covered with a fabulous selection of relaxed slower dishes. Because sometimes life calls for an awesomely delicious slow-cooked roast.

I promise that every recipe will fit these requirements:

1. **Regular ingredients:** They involve simple ingredients that can be found at your regular grocery store. You shouldn't need a trip to a specialty store for anything unless you'd like to take one.

2. **One pot:** Everything here can be cooked in just one pot, or on one griddle, or in one baking dish, or one slow cooker, etc. I tried to keep the mess to a minimum wherever possible.

3. **Kid-friendly:** All of the recipes have been kid-tested and approved. Everyone has a different preference for flavors, but in this book you'll find a distinct absence of some of the most commonly offensive ingredients, such as Brussels sprouts and mushrooms.

4. **Easy swapping:** I want you to make each recipe your own by adding things you love and swapping things for those you don't. The Play With It! notes will get your creative juices flowing.

Our mission is to get families together in the kitchen making food they love. This is your food, take control of it and make it your own.

A NOTE FOR GROWN-UPS

"She won't eat anything but Goldfish crackers!" I remember tearfully wailing to my pediatrician when my daughter was just two years old.

My first baby, my first round at this rodeo of parenting. He chuckled, patted my arm and told me not to lose heart.

"Offer options," he said. "Be patient. This will pass."

No way did I believe him. This doctor surely did not understand that my precious little one was sure to be the first stubborn kid who managed to thrive only on crackers. I thought about my own picky eating history, about my husband's complete aversion to vegetables.

"She's doomed," I moaned.

Our family knows picky eating. We've stared it in the face, and we've eventually learned to call its bluff. But this isn't a before-and-after story. It's an ongoing struggle. We all come into this world with strong preferences. Learning to work with—and around—those preferences is a process that has no endpoint.

Taste buds change, even for adults. I've watched as my own mom has become suddenly averse to certain flavors as she ages. When you learn to have empathy for your children's picky palates, you can put yourself on their team and then cooking your nightly dinner can change from a dreary chore into an exciting challenge. It's a subtle shift that can have an amazing effect on your kids' attitudes toward food.

Remove your children's fears by encouraging adventure and placing control over the recipe in their hands. Let them dictate what goes into the dish as it gets prepared. Have a conversation about what YOU like and don't like. Let them see your own picky preferences. Talk about how you overcame an aversion. What was it that made you eventually come to like that food? When your children can recognize that even Mom and Dad went through taste changes, they become more open-minded that it could happen to them, too.

"I don't like this . . . YET," might just be the most powerful phrase you can encourage in your kitchen.

But what about the TIME?

I know you're groaning, "I don't have time to teach the kids to cook dinner."

Your week is packed. You rush in the door at the end of the long day. Everyone is starving and tired. The last thing you want to do is struggle to make a meal your kids aren't even going to enjoy. The duty of feeding your family feels thankless, and it is just so much easier to grab that frozen entrée or hit the drive-thru.

I've been there. I understand. I have the drive-thru receipts to prove it. I'm not suggesting you get the kids in the kitchen every night. Start small and easy—maybe try a weekend afternoon. Slow things down just a little. Make the experience more about spending the time with your children while you just also happen to be doing something productive that needs to be done.

We only have so many hours in a day. I can't give you an extra hour to add to yours. What I can do is help you to use that one hour to do three amazing things all at one time:

1. Feed your family a meal that will make you feel like you've earned your gold star sticker for the day.

2. Spend quality time learning more about the amazing people your kids are turning into.

3. Encourage solid, lifelong skills that will have an amazing impact on the overall health of your children.

As your children's confidence in the kitchen grows over time, cooking together will become more and more relaxing for all of you.

Imagine the day when you can sit at your kitchen counter and unwind by chatting with your teens as they prepare a meal for you. Maybe you help prep a veggie for them, or maybe you just sit and listen to what's on their mind. They're focusing so much on the routine tasks of dinner that they feel less pressure about opening up because they don't have to look you in the eye while they talk. They're too busy doing something they love and the words just flow.

Invest this effort in your young children now, and make the kitchen a safe place for them to talk to you about whatever is in their heart. Teach them to trust you with the small challenges now so they can come to you with the bigger ones later.

Give them the gift of comfort over a shared meal and they'll relive those memories as they prepare this food well into adulthood. These recipes are food for life.

HEY, KIDS! THIS NOTE'S FOR YOU.

You are awesome. I am so excited that you want to get in the kitchen and learn how to make a meal or two. Wait until you see just how fun it will be!

There are just a few things I want you to know before you get started.

YOU ARE IN CHARGE AND YOUR ADULT HELPER IS SECOND IN COMMAND!

Did you know that in fancy restaurants there's an executive chef who makes the decisions and a sous chef who helps make it all happen? Even in restaurants, it takes two or more chefs to make a meal. It is the job of the leader to make sure their assistant knows what needs to be done. Be kind, and ask for help when you need it. Your adult will be happy to support you as you make your creations.

THIS IS NOT A RULE BOOK. IT IS A PLAY BOOK.

A recipe is just a basic set of instructions that will help you cook the food properly. The ingredients are listed to help you know where to start. But the rules here are made to be bent.

Notice a food that you don't like listed in the ingredients? You can swap it out!

See a pan listed that you don't have? Work with a different one.

Wish it was a little more or less spicy? Adjust the flavor as you like.

This book will give you some creative ideas for changes you can make to the recipes to make them your own, but even those are not the only options. Experiment and play with adding and subtracting whatever you like to a recipe. It's your food, and only you and your family have to enjoy it! That's all that matters.

MAKE A NOTE FOR NEXT TIME.

Did you change something about the recipe and discover that it's your new favorite? Or maybe you tasted it and you wish you had done something differently? Write it down right on that page of the book so you remember next time! This is your book, and you can write on the pages to help you remember anything you need. Maybe even put a star on the recipes that you love the most.

REMEMBER TO KEEP AN OPEN MIND.

Approach your recipes like a taste test challenge. If you don't like it, you can try something different next time. The best way to learn what you do like is to try new things and discover new favorites. My kids were downright shocked to discover they actually do love shrimp and broccoli, but we're still working on liking mashed potatoes and cherry tomatoes. Be sure to read the notes on each recipe. They are written with you in mind to help you find foods that you are most likely to love.

Most importantly, have fun! Play some music while you work. Chat with your parents. Be proud of what you are creating. I wish I could come over and taste it—I know you're going to make great things!

HOW TO USE THIS BOOK:

When I cook recipes from a cookbook, I like to jump around and make what looks tasty to me at that moment. I assume that you will enjoy doing the same. You should know before you begin that the recipes at the beginning of the book are a little easier than the ones toward the end.

To help you get comfortable in the kitchen and make sure you learn all the skills you need to be an excellent home chef, I wrote several skill pages, called "You've Got Skills," that will help highlight things you should know to make each task easier. You will find these pages scattered throughout the book where they are most helpful for the recipes in the chapter.

When you want to cook a recipe, be sure to read it all the way through before you begin. That way, if you see a skill that makes you a little nervous, you can find the detailed information you need on the skill page that matches.

The skills you will learn include:

1. Measuring Dry vs. Wet Ingredients (page 25)
2. Whisking Eggs and Milk (page 31)
3. Playing with Flavor Combinations (page 37)
4. How to Make Scrambled Eggs (page 44)
5. Cutting Food Without a Knife and Beginner Knife-Safety Skills (page 55)
6. Flipping Foods with a Spatula (page 66)
7. How to Broil Chicken Tenderloins (page 81)
8. How to Brown Ground Beef (page 87)
9. Cooking a Large Cut of Meat (page 93)
10. Introduction to Seafood (page 101)
11. How to Sauté Veggies (page 111)
12. Choosing and Cooking Noodles (page 129)
13. How to Make Pizza Dough from Scratch and Roll It Out (page 142)
14. Making the Perfect Pot of Rice (page 159)
15. How to Use an Oven (page 173)
16. Identifying Herbs and Spices (page 191)

Beginner Dinner Tips:
SETTING UP FOR A GREAT TIME
IN THE KITCHEN

PLANNING YOUR MEAL

As fun as it is to imagine, sadly there's no Dinner Fairy who magically stocks your fridge with the ingredients you need to cook your meal. Your job as chef is to plan out what you want to make and ensure that everything you need is ready to go before you start.

Whether you're arranging for just one meal or for a whole week's worth of dinners, most parents call this "meal planning" and it can be the most important step of all.

Meal planning for an entire week means looking at everyone's schedule, deciding which nights are the busiest and need the easiest recipes, and which nights you might have a little more time to play in the kitchen. It can be a complicated task, so start by planning just one meal for a day when you know both you and your adult helper will have some time. That means checking in with their schedule, too!

1. Decide how much time you have available to cook on your planned day and pick a recipe that matches. You don't want to cook a 3-hour pork roast on a day you only have 30 minutes in the kitchen.

2. Choose which meal of the day you will cook. If you're really excited about one of the breakfast ideas but your mornings are always too busy, you could always ask to do breakfast for dinner one night if that works better for your family's schedule.

3. Look at the list of ingredients the recipe needs. Double check inside your fridge and pantry to see what you already have and what you'll need to get from the grocery store. Make sure you have enough of each ingredient, so look at the quantity the recipe calls for.

4. Write down everything you need to buy for the recipe neatly on a piece of paper. Make sure to include how much of the ingredient you need.

5. Think about the rest of the meal you are planning. What else do you need to complete the menu? Would dinner rolls or some garlic bread go well with the recipe you are making? What side dish do you need to complete the dinner? If there aren't a lot of veggies in the recipe, you will definitely want to add a salad, some raw veggies and dip or some fresh fruit to finish the meal. Your sides don't have to be complicated, and most of them can easily be bought ready-to-go from the grocery store. Add what you need to your paper shopping list.

6. Share your shopping list with your adult helper, and ask them nicely to help you get what you need. Offer to go with them and pick out the ingredients yourself if you can.

KEEP IT FUN.

Set the mood for fun in the kitchen. Try turning on some music while you work together. You could even make a playlist of your favorite sing-along tunes to save for cooking time.

Before you get started, check out the list of ingredients. Talk with your helper about the swaps and changes you want to make so everyone is in on the plan.

Make sure everyone has something to do. It's no fun just watching, so be sure to assign a task to each of your helpers.

Pick a recipe that will let you try something new. Maybe it's a new food to taste or a new kitchen tool to try out.

DECIDE WHEN TO SET THE TABLE BEFORE YOU BEGIN.

Is your recipe a quick-fix food or will it have to bake in the oven for a few hours? Chat with your adult helper about whether you think it is a good idea to set your table before you begin cooking or whether you'll have some time at the end to get things ready to eat.

Think about the condiments people will need to enjoy your food. Set out anything you think they will need. Maybe it's salad dressings to go with the salad or the container of grated Parmesan for spaghetti night. When everyone sits down, it's nice to have everything all ready at the table to prevent running back to the kitchen.

SIMPLE SAFETY TIPS TO REMEMBER

1. **Wear an apron.** This keeps your clothing neat, and it also puts another layer between you and hot splatters.

2. **Wear oven mitts.** When you're near anything hot, protect your hands.

3. **Keep your hair tied back.** If you have long hair, pull it back into a ponytail if possible. You don't want your hair to hang in the food or get near the heat of the oven.

4. **Take your time.** More mistakes happen when we rush. Take your time and reread the instructions if you need to. Prep your ingredients first so they are easy to use when they are needed.

5. **Watch your fingers.** No matter what you do, always keep an eye on your fingers and move intentionally.

6. **Ask permission for anything sharp or hot.** Your adult helper will let you know when they feel comfortable with you using a knife or turning the stove burners on and off. Until then, assign those jobs to them.

7. **Be watchful with raw meat.** You don't want to contaminate any other ingredients for your dish by letting raw meat touch other things that won't be cooked. Keep the raw meat separate from everything else, and be sure to clean any surface that it touches before placing new food there.

CLEAN AS YOU GO.

The very first step of cooking any recipe should be filling your sink with hot, soapy water and setting a dish towel out.

After each step of the recipe instructions, look at your work space and consider which tools you are finished using. Rinse them out and swish and give them a quick scrub in the hot soapy water. Rinse and place them on the side of the sink to drip-dry while you move on to the next task.

If you keep this up, almost all of the dishes will already be clean by the time your recipe is finished, and they'll be waiting to be dried and put away for next time. After your meal, you will only have to rinse and clean your dining dishes and the container where the food was cooked.

KEEP YOUR WORKSPACE NEAT.

Pull all of the required ingredients you need from the pantry and fridge. Place them neatly on your counter, and make organized groups for the recipe—all the spices together, all the sauce ingredients together, etc.

As you prep each ingredient, discard the wrapping and produce trimmings in the garbage immediately rather than letting them pile up on your counter.

When you're finished measuring something such as milk or a condiment, return the container to the fridge or pantry immediately. This will help continue to keep your work space clear of clutter.

Take the time to stop and wipe up any spills as they happen to keep your workspace neat.

Set out a plate or bowl to rest your dirty spoons between stirs rather than setting them directly on the counter.

MISTAKES HAPPEN.

When you are learning something new, mistakes are bound to happen. Food will fly across the counter or drop to the floor. Things will come out undercooked or burned. You might forget to add an ingredient that means your muffins won't rise, or you might accidentally put sugar in the dish instead of salt.

It's all ok. I hope you will be able to laugh together about it! These things make excellent stories to share down the road, "Remember the time . . . "

When a mistake happens, simply grab a dish towel and clean up the mess. Own your mistake and keep on trying. You'll do even better next time.

THE BEST KITCHEN TOOLS FOR KIDS

There are so many kitchen tools marketed toward kids these days. Don't be fooled. Just because it's colorful, cute and small, doesn't mean it's a good tool for you to use. Instead, stock your kitchen with our top ten favorites.

1. Manual food processor: Before you're ready to use a grown-up kitchen knife, a manual food processor will help you chop up veggies small enough for use in the recipes. You could also use an electric food processor, but manual ones are much smaller and fit well when stored in your cabinet.

2. Long-handled wooden spoons: The long handle keeps kid hands away from hot food, and the wood won't scratch your nonstick or enamelware pots and pans. When you stick with wood, you don't have to guess which spoon is the "safe one" to use on the cooking dish.

3. Short-handled pots and pans: A long-handled pot or pan can easily get bumped by accident and cause dangerous spills. In my kitchen, we love to use pots and pans that have shorter loop handles for gripping because it keeps them out of the way.

4. Mixing bowl with a handle: Kids can be vigorous stirrers. Use a bowl with a handle and a rubber grip bottom to keep it from sliding off the counter.

5. Sturdy glass measuring cups with easy-read markers: They are one-part measuring tool and one-part mini–mixing bowl. We use these for cracking eggs, melting butter, whisking liquids and as prepped veggie holders. Keep at least one 2-cup (473-ml) and one 4-cup (946-ml) size handy in your stock.

6. Flexible silicone or nylon wide-mouth spatula: These are safe to use on any pot or pan and are the easiest for kids to use to flip foods. They bend a bit and are easy to slip under the food. The wider mouth leaves a bigger surface to hold the food before flipping.

7. Long-handled tongs: The long handle keeps kid hands away from hot foods. Avoid the short-handled ones that tend to be branded for kids.

8. Regular dinner forks and butter knives: Shop your utensil drawer for shorter handled tools that work well for little hands. We use forks for gripping foods to keep fingers away from knives or for moving raw meat onto a pan. Butter knives are a great first knife when cutting butter, cheese or even softer fruits and vegetables.

9. A small step stool: It's not fun to cook if you can't reach! Keep a small stool right in the kitchen for an extra boost.

10. Meat-chopping tool: This little luxury makes preparing ground meats so easy for kids. Can you live without it? Sure. Is taco night way more fun with it? Definitely.

GOOD MORNING, SUNSHINE!

We all start somewhere, and there's no better place to begin than with breakfast. Want to have some fun in the kitchen together? Breakfast is where it's at! Who can resist whipping up a sweet treat in the morning?

Pear-Berry Muffins (page 40), Cinnamon Sugar & Pecan Monkey Bread (page 28), Orange-Blueberry Pancakes (page 34) and Vanilla Spice French Toast (page 32) are the perfect place to learn some simple kitchen skills that will help you with all the recipes in the rest of this book. Once you've mastered baking scones and flipping flapjacks, scrambled eggs and savory breakfast dishes will be the next step toward testing your hand at some new cooking skills.

Our favorite thing about breakfast food is all the mix-and-match combinations you can make. As with everything in this book, these breakfast recipes are meant to be played with. Don't like blueberries? Swap them for chocolate chips in the pancakes! Only have pecans on hand instead of almonds? Those will still taste great in the cherry scones.

What new flavor combinations can you imagine?

You've Got Skills

MEASURING DRY VS. WET INGREDIENTS

Though this may seem like the most obvious thing of all, learning to properly measure your ingredients can make or break your final recipe results. Knowing exactly which tool to use to measure your food and how to do it will give you a really strong start to your kitchen fun.

Every ingredient used in cooking will fall into two categories:

1. **Wet liquids:** milk, juices, water, chicken broth, soy sauce and so on

2. **Dry solids:** flour, sugar, spices, fruit and veggies, nuts and so on

If your ingredient is a wet liquid, you will use a glass measuring cup with marks on the side that tell you how much you've poured into the cup. Your ingredient should meet the line that marks just how much you need. Place your measuring cup on your countertop and read the measuring lines by staring at it straight on, not down. You'll even use this skill in chemistry class someday!

If your ingredient is a dry solid, you use measuring cups with handles that look like scoops. It is important to remember that your ingredient should be even and flat on the top—not rounded like a hill—or you have more of your ingredient than you need. Always use the back of a butter knife to gently even off the top of the cup to make sure you have the just-right amount.

You don't want to pack in the food in a measuring cup, just fill it loosely with your ingredients. The exception to this rule is brown sugar which almost always calls for being packed in tightly. When measuring brown sugar, scoop the sugar with the right measuring cup and then use a spoon or your fingers to squash it down tightly. Keep scooping and packing the sugar until the cup is full and level.

There is one tool we can use for both wet and dry ingredients—our measuring spoons. "Tsp" means a teaspoon. "Tbsp" means a tablespoon. If you see that next to your ingredient, you know to use the measuring spoons whether it is wet or dry. Make sure when you measure a dry ingredient that the spoon is also even and flat. If it's rounded and hilly, you have too much!

EASY CHERRY ALMOND SCONES

This was the first recipe my daughters learned to make all by themselves. The dough is the same even if you play with different flavor combinations. Our favorite part is painting the butter over the tops of the scones before we bake them.

PLAY WITH IT! What other flavors could you put into the 1-cup (237-ml) measuring cup instead of the dried cherries? How about a mix of chocolate chips and pecans? Dried peaches or dried blueberries—mixed with cinnamon chips or by themselves—are yummy, too!

YIELD: 8 TO 12 SCONES

1½ cups (150 g) all-purpose flour

¼ cup (48 g) sugar, plus more for sprinkling

2 tsp (8 g) baking powder

Pinch of salt

1 cup (120 g) dried cherries

⅓ cup (35 g) almond slivers

1 cup (240 ml) heavy cream

¼ tsp almond extract

2 tbsp (28 g) butter

1. HEY KIDS, PLEASE GET US STARTED! ➡️⟶

Set out a cookie sheet, and spray it with cooking spray so your scones won't stick. Ask your adult helper to preheat the oven to 375°F (190°C, or gas mark 5).

Measure the flour and the sugar, and pour them into a large mixing bowl. Measure the baking powder and add it to the bowl. Add a pinch of salt to the bowl, and use your whisk to stir everything together.

Measure the dried cherries. You can decide if you think they are too big. Let your helper chop them up for you if you'd like them a little smaller.

Measure the almond slivers and add them with the cherries to the mixing bowl. Stir all the dry ingredients together so that the dried fruit is coated in flour. This helps make sure they don't all sink to the bottom of the scone when you bake them.

Measure the heavy cream into a liquid measuring cup. Stir the almond extract into the cream; then, pour the mixture into the mixing bowl. Gently stir the cream into the flour. The dough will quickly become very sticky. If it gets too hard to stir with your spatula, it is okay to use your hands to knead the dough. Keep working the dough until there is no more dry flour left in the bowl. You can use your spatula to help scrape up the dried bits at the bottom of the bowl.

Using a large spoon, scoop out a portion of dough and gently form it into a round scone shape with your hands. You should get 8 to 12 scones total depending on how big you make them. Place the scones on the cookie sheet.

2. PARENTS, ⟵ IT'S YOUR TURN!

Place the butter in a microwave-safe bowl, and heat for 5 to 10 seconds until melted.

3. TEAMWORK GETS IT DONE!

Using a pastry brush, paint the melted butter over the top of all the scones. If you don't have a brush, you can drizzle it and spread it using a spoon.

Sprinkle a little sugar over the top of each scone using pinches with your fingers.

Place the scones in the oven. Bake for 15 to 20 minutes until lightly toasted on the top.

CINNAMON SUGAR & PECAN MONKEY BREAD

This monkey bread is a special treat we love to serve on Christmas morning, but it makes for a fun thing to bake any time of year. You'll love pulling apart the sticky, gooey rolls while they're still warm! Don't forget to prep the recipe the night before, so the rolls will rise on your counter overnight.

PLAY WITH IT! The cinnamon pecan flavor is a classic, but you could easily play with the flavors by changing the pudding. How about a vanilla-almond version? Or add your favorite dried fruits such as craisins or dried blueberries.

YIELD: 8 TO 10 SERVINGS

1 tbsp (14 g) softened butter for the pan

½ cup (1 stick [115 g]) butter

1 cup (220 g) loosely packed brown sugar

¼ cup (48 g) granulated sugar

1 tsp cinnamon

1 (3½-oz [96-g]) package of cook-and-serve butterscotch pudding mix (not instant!)

½ cup (60 g) pecans

16–20 frozen round dinner rolls

1. HEY KIDS, PLEASE GET US STARTED!

Using your fingers, rub the tablespoon (14 g) of softened butter all around the inside of a Bundt pan. It's the kind with a hole in the middle! Set the pan aside.

Place the stick of butter in a microwave-safe container and heat for 30 to 40 seconds, until melted. Set aside.

Measure the brown sugar, granulated sugar and cinnamon, and put them in a small bowl. Add the container of pudding mix. Use a fork to combine them all together.

Measure the pecans and either break them up with your fingers or use a manual food processor to chop them up into smaller chunks. Add the pecans to the sugar bowl and stir them together.

Place the frozen dinner rolls in the buttered Bundt pan. Use enough rolls to cover the bottom of your pan. There will be large spaces between the frozen rolls.

Sprinkle the sugared pecan mix evenly over the top of the rolls. Drizzle the melted butter over the top of the rolls, and then place the pan on your counter overnight. Do not cover it because the rolls will rise in the night.

2. PARENTS, IT'S YOUR TURN!

Preheat the oven to 350°F (175°C, or gas mark 4). Bake the rolls for 30 minutes.

3. TEAMWORK GETS IT DONE!

Let the bread rest in the pan for 5 to 10 minutes. Run a butter knife around the edges of the pan. Place your serving platter over the pan, and then holding the two together, flip the pan and plate over so the pan is upside down. Gently wiggle and lift the pan to release the bread onto the platter. If the bread cools too much, everything will stick inside the Bundt pan and you won't be able to flip it out onto a plate.

Serve the bread by pulling apart the rolls or by cutting it into slices.

You've Got Skills

WHISKING EGGS AND MILK

One of the cooking skills that is the most fun to learn is how to use a large whisk to mix eggs and milk. It has always been one of the first things my girls wanted to do when helping in the kitchen. To avoid getting bits of egg all over the counter—and your cabinets—and to keep the eggs inside your recipe, you'll want to follow a few bits of advice.

When we whisk, we are mixing our ingredients together smoothly, but we are also adding air to the mixture. The added air helps scrambled eggs or pancakes get their fluffy, light texture.

1. **Use a big enough bowl.** Pick a large bowl with tall sides so that the vigorous whisking doesn't splash your liquids all over the counter. Our favorite is a large batter bowl with a handle and spout, but any large mixing bowl will do.

   Note: A heavier bowl made of ceramic or glass, rather than thin stainless, is a perfect choice for kids. The added weight will help keep the bowl steady while they practice.

2. **Choose your whisk.** A smaller whisk is perfect for small hands, but we jumped right into the full-size version. Just be sure to only use a wire whisk on glass, plastic or stainless-steel pots and pans, never on nonstick or cast-iron surfaces because it can scratch and ruin the pan. A silicone whisk is the safer option for those, and it can be used on any surface.

3. **Crack your eggs.** Firmly crack your first egg on the side of the bowl, and carefully break open the shell to pour the egg white and yolk into the bowl. If you accidentally get a bit of shell in the bowl, use one of the egg shell halves to scoop out the bits before cracking the next egg.

   Poke each yellow egg yolk with your whisk to break the surface of the yolk. Start making slow circles with the whisk on the bottom of the bowl. Try to keep the whisk in contact with the bottom of the bowl without lifting it up. Slowly speed up your circles while keeping control over the whisk. If you start to splash, you're going too fast!

4. **Mix them up.** When you whisk eggs, you will see the color of the yellow change from dark to light. This is how you know you're getting air into the eggs.

If you need to add milk, whisk the eggs first and then pour the milk into the bowl. Whisk again, until the mixture is fully combined and solid yellow.

VANILLA SPICE FRENCH TOAST

Once you know how to whisk eggs and milk together, the perfect thing to try next is classic French toast. This version has a buttery crispy crust with warm vanilla and cinnamon to give it some spice. This is lovely for a special weekend morning.

PLAY WITH IT! What do you like on top of your French toast? Maple syrup is always delicious, but this dish goes well with strawberry jam or whipped cream, too. In the fall, you could also try hot cinnamon apple slices as garnish.

YIELD: 4 TO 6 SERVINGS

2 tbsp (28 g) butter, plus more for the pan

2 large eggs

1½ cups (355 ml) milk

4 tsp (20 ml) vanilla extract

¼ cup (48 g) sugar

⅔ cup (66 g) all-purpose flour

½ tsp salt

1 tsp cinnamon

¼ tsp nutmeg

1 loaf of challah bread or 1 large round loaf of Hawaiian bread

1. HEY KIDS, PLEASE GET US STARTED!

Set out a 9 x 13-inch (23 x 33-cm) baking dish where you will mix the batter. Place 2 tablespoons (28 g) of butter in a microwave-safe bowl or cup. Heat it for 5 to 10 seconds until it is completely melted. Set the butter aside to cool while you prepare the rest of the batter.

Crack the eggs into your baking dish and gently whisk them. Measure the milk and pour it into the dish. Measure the vanilla extract and add it to the dish. Gently whisk together all the liquid ingredients.

Now measure the sugar and add it to the milk mixture in the dish. Measure the flour. Whisk it gently into the milk and sugar until the batter is completely wet and smooth. Measure the salt, cinnamon and nutmeg, adding them directly to the dish as you go. Whisk them into the mix.

To add the melted butter to the batter, you need to whisk it in carefully so that the heat doesn't scramble the eggs. While whisking the batter with one hand, slowly drizzle the melted butter into the batter with your other hand.

2. PARENTS, IT'S YOUR TURN!

Slice the loaf of challah bread or Hawaiian bread into 1-inch (2.5-cm) thick slices.

Optional: If you want to serve the French toast on one big family platter, preheat the oven to 225°F (110°C, or gas mark ¼) and place a cookie sheet inside. You can keep the French toast you've already griddled warm on the sheet while you finish making the rest of the batch.

In a large skillet, melt 2 tablespoons (28 g) of butter over medium-high heat. When the butter is completely melted and just starting to bubble, the pan is ready for the French toast.

3. TEAMWORK GETS IT DONE!

Finish the French toast in batches of 3 or 4 slices so that you don't overcrowd your hot pan. Carefully dip each slice of bread into the batter so that both sides are completely coated. Let the excess batter drip off over your baking dish before placing it down in the hot pan.

Cook the French toast for 2 minutes on the first side. Use a spatula to flip each piece over and cook for 1 minute. The toast should become golden brown. Place the French toast inside the warm oven while you finish up, or serve each serving immediately. Add 1 tablespoon (14 g) of butter to the pan before adding the next 3 or 4 pieces.

ORANGE–BLUEBERRY PANCAKES

Weekend pancake breakfasts are so special, but if you make enough pancakes at one time, you can refrigerate them to eat on busy school mornings, too! Try a new flavor combination every week, and it will feel like a brand-new breakfast. This makes 24 to 32 small pancakes for a very hungry family or for saving extras for another day.

PLAY WITH IT! Orange–blueberry is our favorite, but you can easily change the flavors. Have you ever tried orange and chocolate together? If you substitute chocolate chips for the blueberries, it's a whole different treat. If you change the orange juice to apple juice, try adding chopped pecans and cinnamon for apple pie pancakes.

YIELD: 24 TO 32 SMALL PANCAKES

2 cups (200 g) all-purpose flour

2 tbsp (24 g) sugar

2 tsp (8 g) baking powder

1 tsp baking soda

1 tsp salt

1½ cups (355 ml) buttermilk

½ cup (118 ml) fresh orange juice

½ tsp almond extract (optional: substitute with vanilla)

2 large eggs

1½ cups (149 g) fresh blueberries or frozen blueberries (thawed and drained)

Butter for the griddle

1. HEY KIDS, PLEASE GET US STARTED!

Measure the flour and add it to a large mixing bowl. Measure the sugar, baking powder, baking soda and salt, and add them to the mixing bowl. Stir the dry ingredients together with a whisk to make sure they are evenly combined.

Measure the buttermilk and orange juice, and pour them directly into the mixing bowl. Measure the almond extract and add that to the bowl. Carefully crack the eggs into the measuring cup you used for the buttermilk, so you can check for bits of shell you might miss. Use a fork to break the yolks and whisk the eggs until they are smooth and yellow. Pour them into the mixing bowl.

Use a spatula to stir together the pancake batter until there is no more dry flour and everything is smooth and wet. Don't forget to scrape the bottom of the bowl for any dry flour you've missed. Gently stir in the blueberries until they are evenly spread throughout the batter.

2. PARENTS, IT'S YOUR TURN!

Heat the griddle to medium-high heat. Melt a tablespoon or two (14 to 28 g) of butter so that the surface is coated.

OPTIONAL: Preheat the oven to 225°F (110°C, or gas mark ¼) and place a cookie sheet inside. You can store the finished pancakes in here to keep warm while you finish the rest of the batch, so you can serve them family-style.

3. TEAMWORK GETS IT DONE!

Use a ¼-cup (60-ml) measuring cup to portion out the pancakes. Drop scoops of batter onto the preheated griddle. The batter will spread, so leave room between the pancakes. You know it is time to flip the pancakes when you see air bubbles popping evenly over the surface of the pancake. Use a spatula to flip them over and cook until golden brown, about 2 to 3 minutes per side.

Add an additional tablespoon or two (14 to 29 g) of butter to the griddle between batches of pancakes. Serve immediately.

TO STORE: Pancakes can be stored in single layers separated by waxed paper in the refrigerator. To reheat, place them in your toaster and they'll get nice crispy edges.

You've Got Skills

PLAYING WITH FLAVOR COMBINATIONS

One of the most fun things about cooking is playing with the flavors to make a recipe your very own invention. Everything in this book is a simple place for you to start, and then you can add the things you love most to each of your dishes.

There Is NO Failing in Cooking!

You need to know that there is no such thing as failing in cooking. Even if your recipe doesn't turn out the way you want, you've learned something. Make a note in your book, and change it up again the next time!

1. Learn what you DO like. First, you need to learn which foods you like and which ones you are still learning to like. We think it is a great idea to try each recipe in this book as it is written the first time you make it. Then, talk with your family about what you like and what you might like to see more of, less of, or instead of in the list of ingredients. Make notes right on the recipe page for next time!

2. Add one thing that you love. When you start to play with the recipe the next time you make it, it might be easiest to simply try adding something new into the dish. For example, in the Pumpkin Patch Waffles (page 38) you could add craisins, butterscotch chips or both! Did you like this version even better? Write it down!

3. Swap just one thing. Next, you might try swapping out one or two ingredients and adding something different. When you first try it, look for swaps where your new ingredient is similar to the one you are replacing: a veggie for a veggie, a fruit for a fruit. Maybe in the Tex-Mex Sweet Potato and Sausage Skillet (page 48) you would rather have a regular potato, or you want to change the Pear–Berry Muffins (page 40) from pears and raspberries to blueberries and almonds.

4. Swap out lots of things. The most adventurous step to making a recipe your own is to change the flavor completely. For example, you can take the Mexican-flavored sweet potato skillet on page 48 and turn it into an Italian potato hash by changing the seasonings, the vegetables you use, and the flavor of cheese from cheddar to mozzarella. The main steps for making it will be exactly the same, but by switching the spices and some of the ingredients, you've turned it into something completely new and completely yours.

PUMPKIN PATCH WAFFLES

We used to buy frozen waffles until we tried this delicious homemade version. They are so much better than anything you'll find at the grocery store! It makes a large batch of 20 to 22 waffles so that you'll have plenty of leftovers to get you through a busy school week.

PLAY WITH IT! This recipe is really easy to play with! Start with the plain pumpkin recipe and imagine what you could mix in to go with it: butterscotch chips, chopped pecans, diced apples, dried cranberries. Just mix in ½ to 1 cup (60 to 120 g) of any combination you like after the batter has been mixed together.

YIELD: 20 TO 22 WAFFLES

4 tbsp (57 g) butter

2½ cups (248 g) all-purpose flour

¼ cup (55 g) packed brown sugar

2 tsp (8 g) baking powder

4 tsp (16 g) pumpkin pie spice

½ tsp baking soda

½ tsp salt

2½ cups (592 ml) buttermilk

4 large eggs

1 cup (180 g) canned pumpkin

1. HEY KIDS, PLEASE GET US STARTED!

Put the butter in a microwave-safe container and heat for 10 to 20 seconds, until melted. Set aside to cool while you prepare the batter.

Measure the flour and add it to a large mixing bowl. Measure out the brown sugar, baking powder, pumpkin pie spice, baking soda and salt. Add them to the mixing bowl. Whisk all the dry ingredients together so they are evenly combined.

Measure the buttermilk and add it to the mixing bowl. Carefully crack the eggs into the same measuring cup you used for the buttermilk. Watch for any bits of shell you might miss. Use a fork to break the yolks, and whisk together the eggs until smooth and yellow. Add the eggs to the mixing bowl.

Measure the pumpkin and add it to the mixing bowl. Stir together the batter until it is evenly combined and smooth. While stirring the batter with a spoon in one hand, slowly pour the melted butter into the batter.

2. PARENTS, IT'S YOUR TURN!

Preheat a waffle iron, and spray it with cooking spray. Pour the servings of batter into the waffle iron and cook according to the directions on your machine.

OPTIONAL: Preheat the oven to 225°F (110°C, or gas mark ¼) and place a cookie sheet inside. You can store the finished waffles in here to keep warm while you finish the rest of the batch, so you can serve them family-style.

3. TEAMWORK GETS IT DONE!

Remove the waffles from the waffle iron with long-handled tongs to keep your hands safe. Keep the waffles warm in the oven to eat family-style, or serve them immediately.

To freeze them, allow the waffles to cool to room temperature. Store them in an airtight baggie with pieces of waxed paper in between to keep them from sticking.

PEAR–BERRY MUFFINS

Muffins are a perfect way to begin baking together. These simple treats can be mixed up to make any flavor you could imagine. The batter is simple, the rest is up to you!

PLAY WITH IT! You have 1½ cups of space to play! What else could you use here instead of the pear and raspberries? How about 1 cup (100 g) of blueberries and ½ cup (52 g) of almond slivers? You could try diced apples, peaches, pineapple, blackberries, pecans, walnuts or chocolate chips, too.

NOTE: The recipe calls for pumpkin pie spice to make your baking easier—you don't have to measure out each spice. Surprise, there's no pumpkin inside! It's just a common blend of cinnamon, ginger, nutmeg and allspice that's commonly used for baking pumpkin pie.

YIELD: 1 DOZEN MUFFINS

½ cup (1 stick [115 g]) butter

2 cups (200 g) all-purpose flour

1 tbsp (11 g) baking powder

½ tsp salt

½ tsp pumpkin pie spice

⅔ cup (147 g) packed brown sugar

1 cup (237 ml) milk

2 large eggs

1 tsp vanilla extract

1 fresh pear

½ cup (50 g) fresh raspberries (or frozen, thawed and drained)

2 tbsp (24 g) granulated sugar

Cinnamon, for sprinkling (optional)

1. HEY KIDS, PLEASE GET US STARTED! ➤⟶

Add the butter to a microwave-safe container and heat for 25 to 30 seconds, until melted. Set aside to cool while you prepare the batter.

Line a muffin tin with wrappers and set aside.

Measure the flour and add it to a large mixing bowl. Measure the baking powder, salt, pumpkin pie spice and brown sugar. Add them to the mixing bowl. Use a whisk to stir together the dry ingredients to make sure they are evenly combined.

Measure the milk and pour it into the mixing bowl. Carefully crack the eggs into the same cup you used for the milk. Watch for any bits of shell you missed. Use a fork to break the yolks, and whisk the eggs until they are smooth and yellow. Pour them into the mixing bowl.

Add the vanilla extract and butter to the bowl, and gently stir the batter until there is no more dry flour.

2. PARENTS, ⟵◄ IT'S YOUR TURN!

Preheat the oven to 400°F (200°C, or gas mark 6).

Wash and peel the pear. Cut it into small diced pieces. Carefully wash and dry the fresh raspberries, and cut them into halves or quarters.

3. TEAMWORK GETS IT DONE!

Gently fold the fruit into the muffin batter. Using a large scoop or spoon, evenly add the batter to the muffin tin. Sprinkle the granulated sugar over the top of the muffins. Optional: A little sprinkle of cinnamon is also delicious on the top!

Bake for 15 to 17 minutes, until a toothpick inserted in 1 or 2 of the muffins comes out clean.

BERRY DELICIOUS GRANOLA YOGURT PARFAITS

Homemade granola can be an excellent after-school snack all by itself, or you can use it for fancy yogurt parfaits for a special breakfast or treat. Pick your favorite flavor of yogurt and sprinkle the granola along with your favorite fresh fruits for a healthy and filling meal.

PLAY WITH IT! You can swap the pecans and raisins for any combination of nut and dried fruit you enjoy. How about almonds and peaches? Dried coconut and mangoes? Pistachios and craisins? What mix will you love most?

YIELD: 8 PARFAITS

2 cups (322 g) old-fashioned oats

¼ cup (30 g) pecans

¼ cup (55 g) packed brown sugar

¼ cup (38 g) raisins

1 tbsp (8 g) cinnamon

¼ cup (60 ml) canola oil

2 tbsp (30 ml) honey

2 tbsp (30 ml) maple syrup

½ tsp vanilla extract

1 (32-oz [946-ml]) container vanilla yogurt

2 cups (200 g) fresh berries, washed

1. HEY KIDS, PLEASE GET US STARTED!

Measure the old-fashioned oats and pour them into a large mixing bowl. Measure the pecans, brown sugar, raisins and cinnamon. Add them to the mixing bowl. Stir everything together with a large spoon.

Measure the canola oil, honey, maple syrup and vanilla extract. Add them each directly to the mixing bowl. Stir everything together with your spoon until the mixture is evenly combined and everything is coated and wet.

Pour the granola out onto a large cookie sheet, and spread it into an even layer.

2. PARENTS, IT'S YOUR TURN!

Preheat the oven to 325°F (170°C, or gas mark 3). Bake the granola for 25 to 30 minutes until lightly toasted. Stir the batch 2 or 3 times while baking to prevent burning.

3. TEAMWORK GETS IT DONE!

Set the granola aside to cool. Once it is cool enough to touch, break the granola into smaller chunks, and store it in an airtight container for up to 2 weeks.

To assemble the parfaits, you need about ½ cup (123 g) of yogurt, ¼ cup (25 g) of berries and ¼ cup (20 g) of the cooled granola for each parfait. In a small mason jar or pretty glass, use a spoon to scoop and layer half of the yogurt, half of the berries and half of the granola. Then repeat the layers with the remaining portions.

Only assemble the parfaits when you plan to eat them. The granola will get soggy if stored with the fruit and yogurt in the fridge.

You've Got Skills

HOW TO MAKE SCRAMBLED EGGS

Learning to scramble eggs on the stove top is the perfect introduction to cooking. This is the first thing I taught my girls to do when they wanted more responsibility in the kitchen. Not only do they make a yummy breakfast all by themselves, but you can add scrambled eggs to a variety of ingredients to make a hearty meal for breakfast, lunch or dinner!

Scrambled eggs are perfect for feeding a hungry crowd or just one hungry kid. You can adjust the amount of eggs in the pan for the number of people you want to feed, but the instructions are exactly the same for how to cook them.

1. Prepare the eggs and your tools. Decide how many eggs you want to cook, 1 or 2 per person. Crack the eggs into a large mixing bowl and whisk them until they are light yellow. Optional: Sometimes we whisk in 1 tablespoon (15 ml) of milk to the eggs to make them extra fluffy.

Now, set out your tools. A large shallow skillet works best for scrambling 4 or more eggs. If you are making just 1 to 3 eggs, use a smaller shallow skillet. A long-handled wooden spoon is the best choice for scrambling eggs. While learning this skill, it is useful to wear oven mitts on both hands and use a long-handled spoon.

Place your pan on a stove-top burner, and turn the heat on to medium-high. Add 1 tablespoon (14 g) of butter to the pan and let it melt. When the butter starts to make bubbles and foam on the top, the pan is hot enough.

2. Add the eggs. Pour the egg mixture into the pan, and place the dirty bowl in the sink. Using your wooden spoon, stir the eggs slowly while making gentle figure-eight strokes.

3. Keep stirring! The eggs will start to curdle together; continue making figure-eight strokes until there is no more liquid on the bottom of the pan.

4. Flip to finish. Gently flip and nudge the fluffy eggs, making sure their surface is fully cooked and not wet. Use your spoon to break up any pieces that are too big. Sprinkle some fresh chopped chives or green onions on top, if you'd like. Serve immediately; scrambled eggs get cold fast and do not reheat well.

PRETEND HUEVOS RANCHEROS

Real huevos rancheros are made with fried eggs and some complicated sauces. In our house, we love Mexican food so much that my daughter decided to make her own version of this classic dish in an easier way that we can enjoy any time. The best part is that it's a little bit like having tacos for breakfast! This makes two servings, but the recipe is very flexible. Just add more eggs and tortillas if you have more hungry mouths to feed.

PLAY WITH IT! Whatever you like on your tacos goes great here. You can add onions, peppers, corn and beans right into the skillet before you cook your eggs, or top them with fresh tomatoes, green onions, shredded cheese or hot sauce. Just take your pick!

YIELD: 2 SERVINGS

2 tortillas, corn or flour

1 (16-oz [454-g]) jar prepared salsa

1 (16-oz [890-ml]) container sour cream

4 eggs

1 tbsp (14 g) butter

1. HEY KIDS, PLEASE GET US STARTED!

Place the tortillas on a microwave-safe plate, and place them inside the microwave. You'll heat these up later on, just before serving.

Place a spoon in the jar of salsa and another in the container of sour cream, and put them at the table for serving.

Crack the eggs into a small mixing bowl. Whisk them until smooth and light yellow.

2. PARENTS, IT'S YOUR TURN!

Place a skillet over medium-high heat. Add the butter and let it melt.

3. TEAMWORK GETS IT DONE!

Scramble the eggs in the skillet. Once they are firm, heat the tortillas for 15 to 20 seconds in the microwave.

To serve: Place 1 tortilla on each of the 2 plates. Top the tortillas with the scrambled eggs, equally divided between the 2 servings. Top the eggs with the salsa and a dollop of sour cream. You can eat it rolled up burrito-style or enjoy it as an open-faced meal with a fork and knife.

TEX-MEX SWEET POTATO AND SAUSAGE SKILLET

Some mornings call for a really hearty breakfast. This is exactly what you need when you have a big day ahead! Savory sausage combined with sweet potatoes topped with salsa will stick to your ribs.

PLAY WITH IT! Though this recipe tastes a lot like a Mexican dish, you can change the seasonings to make it your own. For an Italian version, use dried thyme and garlic powder instead of the cumin and chili powder, try fresh tomatoes and peppers instead of the salsa, and top with mozzarella.

YIELD: 4 SERVINGS

2 tsp (8 g) chili powder

1 tsp cumin

4 eggs

½ small red onion

1 medium sweet potato

3 tbsp (45 ml) olive oil

½ lb (227 g) bulk breakfast sausage (sweet Italian sausage also works great)

½ cup (20 g) fresh parsley

1 cup (259 g) prepared salsa

1 tbsp (14 g) butter

1. HEY KIDS, PLEASE GET US STARTED! ➤━━━➤

Measure the chili powder and cumin, and place them in a small cup near the stove.

Crack the eggs into a small bowl. Whisk them until they are smooth and light yellow.

2. PARENTS, ◄━━━◄ IT'S YOUR TURN!

Chop the onion into small diced pieces. You can also let kids do this with a manual food processor—see You've Got Skills on page 55, if needed.

Wash and peel the sweet potato. Cut it in half lengthwise, and then slice it into thin half moons. Chop the parsley and set aside.

Place a large skillet over medium-high heat.

3. TEAMWORK GETS IT DONE!

Add the olive oil to the skillet. Add the onions and sweet potatoes to the skillet, and stir them to coat in the oil. Spread them into an even layer, and let them cook for 2 to 3 minutes. Toss the potatoes, and then let sit for another 2 to 3 minutes. Continue tossing and cooking until the potatoes are tender, about 15 to 18 minutes.

Have the adult helper transfer the hot potatoes to a plate. Add the bulk sausage to the pan. Use a spoon to crumble up the sausage as it cooks, about 3 to 4 minutes. Once the sausage is no longer pink, add the spices and stir to combine. Cook the sausage with the seasonings for 1 minute, and then return the potato mixture to the pan. Stir to combine the sausage and potatoes.

Add the salsa and fresh parsley, and stir. Pour the potato mixture onto a large serving platter. Loosely cover the platter with a sheet of tinfoil to keep everything warm while you prepare the eggs.

Have your adult helper wipe clean the skillet and place it back over medium-high heat. Add the tablespoon (14 g) of butter and let it melt. Scramble the eggs in the skillet.

To serve, place the eggs on top of the potato mixture, and divide it up to make 4 servings.

CHEESY HAM & BROCCOLI BREAKFAST PIE

This breakfast pie, or quiche, if you like its fancier name, is delicious when served warm or even at room temperature. It also makes a great lunch or dinner if you serve it with some fresh fruit and a simple salad.

PLAY WITH IT! Quiche comes in endless varieties of flavors! Almost any meat and veggie combination you can think of would work here. Some fun combinations to get you started: A) sausage, tomato, bell peppers and mozzarella; B) chicken, asparagus and Swiss cheese; and C) spicy turkey, jalapeño peppers, tomato and cheddar cheese.

YIELD: 6 SERVINGS

1 (14.1-oz [399-g]) package of refrigerated pie crust

1 cup (230 g) frozen broccoli florets

3 eggs

1 cup (237 ml) milk

1 tbsp (16 g) Dijon mustard

½ lb (227 g) deli ham

2 cups (222 g) shredded Colby Jack cheese

½ tsp pepper

1. HEY KIDS, PLEASE GET US STARTED!

The refrigerated pie crust dough needs to sit on your counter for 10 to 15 minutes before you can work with it. Set it out to warm up a little while you prepare the pie filling.

Heat the frozen broccoli according to the instructions on the package, usually about 4 to 5 minutes in the microwave. Drain any excess water that may have collected in the bag while cooking.

Crack the eggs into a mixing bowl and gently whisk them. Measure the milk, and pour it in with the eggs. Add the Dijon mustard, and use a whisk to combine the eggs and milk until the mixture is smooth.

Ask your adult helper to chop the broccoli and deli ham up. Stir the broccoli and ham pieces in with the eggs. Measure the shredded cheese and pepper, add them to the eggs and stir it all up.

2. PARENTS, IT'S YOUR TURN!

When your kid chef asks, chop the broccoli and deli ham into small, bite-size chunks.

Preheat the oven to 350°F (175°C, or gas mark 4).

3. TEAMWORK GETS IT DONE!

Roll the pie crust dough into a 9-inch (23-cm) pie plate or a 10-inch (26-cm) quiche dish. Kids will enjoy pinching the edges of the crust to form the pie. Use a fork to prick the bottom of the crust all over. This will prevent bubbles forming in the crust.

Pour the egg mixture into the pie dish. Use a spoon to make sure all the chunky ingredients are evenly spread out throughout the pie.

Bake for 60 minutes, until the eggs are set and the crust is golden brown.

MIX AND MATCH: SOUP & SAMMIES

Creative lunches are easier when you can pick one soup and one sandwich and make endless combinations. Could you just make one or the other? Totally, but they are always better together. To keep things easy, you could always make a big batch of soup with bread or crackers one day and enjoy the leftovers with a freshly made sandwich on the second day.

These one pot soups are the perfect base for your imagination. Toss a little of this and a little of that in with the recipes, and you'll have your very own invention. They make nice big batches, so you'll have plenty left over to fill a Thermos and bring to school for your own lunch!

The sandwiches are perfect for dunking into your soup of choice, and they make a wonderful treat all on their own for a weekend or busy evening dinner with some fresh fruit or raw veggies.

Large Chunks

Small Pieces

Half Moons

Bite Sized Pieces

You've Got Skills

CUTTING FOOD WITHOUT A KNIFE AND BEGINNER KNIFE-SAFETY SKILLS

Every parent has a different idea about when it is safe to let kids use knives in the kitchen. For the recipes in this book, we want you to be able to prepare the dish with or without a knife in case your parent isn't ready yet for you to start using them. Here you'll find instructions for both: how to use a manual food processor, along with tips for getting comfy with basic knife skills! These clever tricks will help you prepare food like a pro.

Kid-Friendly Tools for Cutting Food

Manual food processor: This handy tool is our favorite for chopping up most veggies. Pop the food inside, place the lid on top, and when you pump the handle your fingers are nice and safe from the cutting blades. The only problem is you can't drop a whole onion, pepper, tomato, etc. into the processor. You'll need a helper to cut the whole vegetable into large chunks first.

Scissors: Many soft foods, particularly canned whole tomatoes, can be "chopped" up by simply using a clean pair of kitchen scissors. Once you've opened the can, you can cut the tomatoes right inside of it.

Butter knife: For soft fruits and veggies or for bits of chicken or cheese, we'll use the butter knife from our regular tableware to prepare food for the recipes. It's a great first step toward using a regular kitchen knife and can often cut through most things.

Always, always keep your fingers away from the tool you are using to cut. Go slowly, and keep control of your tools at all times.

Do your parents think you're ready to use a knife?

A note to parents: When your child is ready to begin using a real kitchen knife, start with the small paring knife from your kitchen set. The smaller knife is far easier for kids to control and is perfect for cutting carrots, onions, and more. Make sure the knife is nice and sharp, even though that may feel a little scary. Dull knives take more work to cut through the food and are a main cause of kitchen accidents.

1. Hold the knife carefully! Never pick up a knife by the blade. Always hold it on the handle.

2. Go SLOWLY, and do not take your eyes off the knife when you are cutting.

3. Keep your fingers that are holding the food you are cutting away from the blade at all times. If your food becomes too small to hold and still cut safely, ask your parent to finish up the last few cuts.

4. Use a sawing action to slice through the food rather than just pressing straight down. This will work the sharp blade safely into the food, so it doesn't accidentally slip.

5. The most commonly used cut sizes used in this book are featured in the photos for your reference.

CONFETTI VEGGIE SOUP

Now that you've learned some tricks to cut food, this soup is the perfect recipe to practice your skills! Which veggies are more fun to chop than the others? If you see something suspicious in the list of veggies, feel free to swap it with something you like better!

PLAY WITH IT! Almost any vegetable you can imagine would go great inside of this tomato-based soup: peppers, corn, potatoes, peas or spinach would all be great mix-ins. The trick is to just be sure everything is cut up into nice small pieces, which are easier for everyone to eat. You could also add small chunks of cooked chicken or a sprinkle of Parmesan cheese.

YIELD: 8 SERVINGS

1 medium onion

4 celery ribs

2 zucchini

1 cup (145 g) fresh green beans

1 (28-oz [794-g]) can of whole tomatoes

4 carrots

2 tbsp (30 ml) olive oil

3 tsp (9 g) jarred minced garlic

Salt & pepper

1 tsp dried oregano

1 tsp dried basil

6 cups (1.4 L) chicken stock

1. HEY KIDS, PLEASE GET US STARTED! ➤➤➤

Have your helper cut the onion into quarters so you can chop it up in a manual food processor.

Use a butter knife to cut the celery, zucchini and green beans into small chunks.

Open the can of whole tomatoes with a can opener, and use your kitchen scissors to cut them up into very small pieces right inside the can. If you don't have kitchen scissors, you can use a slotted spoon to carefully scoop the tomatoes out of the juices onto a plate and cut them with your butter knife. Set aside the plate of tomatoes.

2. PARENTS, ⬅⬅ IT'S YOUR TURN!

Chop the carrots into small pieces.

Put a soup pot over medium-high heat.

3. TEAMWORK GETS IT DONE!

Add the olive oil to the soup pot. Once it is heated, add the onion, celery, carrots and minced garlic to the pot. Sprinkle it with a bit of salt and pepper, and stir to combine.

When the onions have turned translucent (clear) after 4 to 5 minutes, add the oregano, basil, zucchini and green beans to the pot. Stir and cook for 3 to 4 minutes until the veggies are tender.

Pour the tomatoes into the pot along with the chicken stock. Stir the soup and cover it with a lid. When the mixture comes to a gentle boil, turn the heat down to low and let simmer for 20 minutes.

All the chefs in the kitchen should carefully take a test taste of the soup—watch out, it will be hot! Now is the time to add more salt or spices so that it tastes just right to you. Work together to season it the way you love.

NOTE: The leftovers are even more delicious when the flavors have had a chance to hang out together!

WAY BETTER THAN CANNED TOMATO BASIL SOUP

Tomato soup goes with grilled cheese like hot fudge goes with ice cream. You absolutely need the best tomato soup for dunking your best grilled cheese! This homemade version is so much yummier than the canned variety and makes a nice large pot so everyone in the family can enjoy a big bowl.

PLAY WITH IT! This basic tomato soup can be used as the starter recipe for even fancier versions, just use your imagination! You can add bell peppers or squash, change the seasonings to cumin and chipotle pepper for a spicier version, or top it with your favorite shredded cheese.

YIELD: 4 TO 6 SERVINGS

1 small onion

1 tbsp (2 g) dried basil

½ tsp sugar

1 bay leaf

4 tbsp (57 g) butter

2 tsp (6 g) jarred minced garlic

Pinch of salt

1 (28-oz [794-g]) can diced tomatoes

1½ cups (355 ml) chicken stock

1. HEY KIDS, PLEASE GET US STARTED! ➤━━➤

Have your helper cut the onion into 4 large pieces so you can finish chopping it up using a manual food processor.

Measure the basil and sugar, and put them in a small bowl. Add the bay leaf to the bowl, and set it by the stove.

Measure the butter, and hand it to your adult helper.

2. PARENTS, ←━━ IT'S YOUR TURN!

Add the butter to a large soup pot, and turn the heat on to medium-high.

3. TEAMWORK GETS IT DONE!

When the butter has melted, add the chopped onions. Measure and add the garlic and pinch of salt to the pot, and stir to combine. Cook the onions until they turn translucent (clear), about 3 to 5 minutes.

Add the tomatoes, chicken stock, basil, bay leaf and sugar to the pot, and stir to combine. Cook the soup until it starts to bubble, then put a lid on top of the pot and have your helper turn the heat to low. Cook the soup for 25 minutes.

Remove the bay leaf from the pot and discard. Use an immersion blender to puree the soup until smooth, being very careful to not lift it out of the soup while it is turned on. If you don't have one, have your adult helper transfer the soup to a traditional blender and puree.

All the chefs in the kitchen should carefully take a test taste of the soup—watch out, it will be hot! Now is the time to add more salt or some pepper so that it tastes just right to you. Work together to season it the way you love.

COUNTRY CAPTAIN CHICKEN SOUP

This spicy chicken soup is the perfect way to introduce some new, super delicious flavors. Garam marsala is a blend that has many familiar spices such as cinnamon, cloves and nutmeg, and also mixes in new ones such as coriander, cardamom and caraway. The chopped-up green apple is a fun sweet surprise.

PLAY WITH IT! We love to top this soup with sour cream and a little fresh cilantro. It would also be delicious with a circle of crunchy toasted bread and some melted cheese, served like a French onion soup.

NOTE: This is a perfect Instant Pot® recipe if you have one. Just sauté the ingredients right in the Instant Pot, and then add everything but the sour cream and cilantro and set for 20 minutes on the Soup setting.

YIELD: 6 TO 8 SERVINGS

1 small yellow onion

1 red pepper

1 tbsp (15 g) garam marsala

1 tsp dried ginger

¼ tsp cayenne pepper

¼ cup (46 g) orzo

2 tbsp (19 g) currants (or raisins)

Sour cream, for serving

1 green apple

½ cup (20 g) fresh cilantro

1 tbsp (15 ml) olive oil

4 tsp (13 g) jarred minced garlic

28 oz (794 g) crushed tomatoes

5 cups (1.2 L) chicken stock

1½ lb (680 g) boneless, skinless chicken thighs

1. HEY KIDS, PLEASE GET US STARTED!

Have your helper cut the onion into 4 large quarters. Then ask your helper to open and remove the seeds of the red pepper so you can chop the onion and pepper up into small pieces in a manual food processor.

Measure the seasonings—the garam marsala, ginger and cayenne pepper—into a small cup. Set them aside near the stove.

Measure the orzo and currants, and place them in small bowls near the stove.

Place a spoon in the container of sour cream, and put it on the table for serving later.

2. PARENTS, IT'S YOUR TURN!

While your child is chopping the onions and peppers, core and dice the green apple.

Wash and chop the cilantro, and set aside for serving.

3. TEAMWORK GETS IT DONE!

Put a large soup pot over medium-high heat, and drizzle in the olive oil. Add the chopped onions and peppers, then measure and add the minced garlic. Sauté until the onions are translucent, about 5 minutes. Add the seasonings, and stir the veggies around until everything is coated. Cook for 1 minute.

Add the crushed tomatoes and the chicken stock, and stir the mixture to combine. Add the chicken thighs and chopped apples, and bring the pot to a gentle boil. Cover the pot with a lid and turn the heat down to low. Simmer the soup for 20 minutes.

Using a slotted spoon, remove the chicken thighs and place them on a plate. Using a fork and butter knife to keep your hands away from the hot meat, cut the thighs into small bite-size chunks and return them to the pot. Add the orzo and currants to the soup and simmer for another 7 minutes.

Serve the soup with a dollop of sour cream and a sprinkle of the fresh cilantro.

OOEY GOOEY CHEESY LASAGNA SOUP

As yummy as a big pan of lasagna can be, this soup is a whole lot easier to make! The gooey melted cheese on top is irresistible. If you don't want to make a sandwich to go with it, a basket full of warm breadsticks would be just perfect.

PLAY WITH IT! Do you like things a little zestier? This is made with ground beef, but spicy Italian bulk sausage would be delicious instead. You can also find spicier marinara blends to kick it up. Chopped zucchini or sweet corn would be yummy mix-ins, or you could change the shape of the pasta noodle and make it a chunkier stew.

YIELD: 6 TO 8 SERVINGS

1 small onion

2 tsp (6 g) jarred minced garlic

2 tsp (1 g) oregano

1 tsp dried basil

½ tsp crushed red pepper

1 tbsp (15 ml) olive oil

1 lb (454 g) lean ground beef

1 (24-oz [656-ml]) jar marinara sauce

5 cups (1 L) chicken stock

2 bay leaves

½ cup (92 g) orzo

1 cup (40 g) baby spinach

½ cup (90 g) shredded Parmesan

1 cup (130 g) shredded mozzarella, for serving

1. HEY KIDS, PLEASE GET US STARTED! ➤——→

Have your helper cut the onion into quarters so you can chop it up into small pieces with a manual food processor.

Measure the garlic, oregano, basil and crushed red pepper flakes, and mix them in a small bowl. Set it next to the stove.

2. PARENTS, ←—— IT'S YOUR TURN!

Place a large soup pot over medium-high heat. Add the olive oil and ground beef.

3. TEAMWORK GETS IT DONE!

Brown the beef, breaking it up into small pieces with a long-handled spoon. If the adult helper approves, you can help stir the beef while it's cooking. When it is no longer pink, about 5 minutes, have the adult helper drain any excess fat out of the pot.

Return the pot to the heat and add the minced garlic and dried seasonings to the beef. Stir and cook for 1 minute more. Pour the marinara sauce into the pot, and stir to combine. Measure and pour the chicken stock into the pot, and stir again. When the mixture starts to bubble, add the bay leaves and reduce the heat to low. Cover the pot with a lid and let it simmer for 10 minutes.

Measure and add the orzo pasta directly to the pot. Stir and cover the pot again. Simmer for another 10 minutes until the pasta is tender. Remove the bay leaves and throw them away.

Measure and add the baby spinach and shredded Parmesan to the soup, and stir. The heat will wilt the spinach and melt the cheese quickly.

All the chefs in the kitchen should carefully take a test taste of the soup—watch out, it will be hot! Now is the time to add any salt or some pepper so that it tastes just right to you. Remember that the Parmesan cheese added saltiness, so you may not need any extra salt.

Serve immediately with a sprinkle of mozzarella cheese over the top of each bowl.

GREEK LEMON DROP CHICKEN SOUP

This simple chicken soup is the perfect solution when you're feeling under the weather. It's warm and comforting with plenty of chicken and noodles, and it has a thick and creamy broth thanks to the addition of an egg. We love the brightness of the lemon, but you could easily leave that out if you prefer.

PLAY WITH IT! Simple light vegetables would go best with this soup. You could add peas, zucchini or chunks of asparagus if you like. You could also add a little garlic to the pot when you brown the chicken. If you want to play with some seasonings, oregano, basil or thyme are all great additions.

YIELD: 6 TO 8 SERVINGS

6 cups (1.4 L) chicken stock

1 tbsp (15 ml) olive oil

1½ lb (680 g) boneless, skinless chicken thighs

Salt & pepper

¾ cup (121 g) orzo pasta

1 egg

1 lemon

¼ cup (12 g) fresh chives

1. HEY KIDS, PLEASE GET US STARTED! ➤

Measure the chicken stock while you have your helper put a large soup pot over medium-high heat. Ask your helper to add the olive oil and chicken thighs to the pot. Sprinkle them with salt and pepper, and let them cook for 3 to 4 minutes.

If your adult helper approves, use a long-handled pair of tongs to flip the chicken over so the other side can cook for another 3 minutes.

Add the chicken stock to the pot, and continue to cook until the mixture comes to a bubble. Cover the pot with a lid and reduce the heat to low. Cook for 10 minutes.

Measure out the orzo pasta, add it into the soup and cook for another 10 minutes.

Meanwhile, crack the egg into a measuring cup. Then wash and cut the lemon in half with a butter knife and squeeze the juice into the same cup. Use a fork to whisk the egg and lemon juice until smooth, light yellow and slightly frothy.

2. PARENTS, IT'S YOUR TURN!

Assist your kid chef with sautéing the chicken thighs when asked.

Chop the fresh chives and set aside.

Ladle 1 cup (237 ml) of the hot soup broth into a large mixing bowl. With a whisk in one hand and the measuring cup full of lemon-egg mixture in the other, slowly drizzle the lemon mixture into the hot broth while vigorously whisking at the same time. This will temper the egg and prevent it from scrambling in the soup.

Pour the eggy broth back into the big pot of soup and stir.

3. TEAMWORK GETS IT DONE!

Use a slotted spoon to remove the chicken thighs to a large plate. Use a fork and butter knife to break them up into bite-size pieces. Return the chicken and juices back to the pot and stir.

All the chefs in the kitchen should carefully take a test taste of the soup—watch out, it will be hot! Now is the time to add more salt or some pepper so that it tastes just right to you. Work together to season it the way you love.

Serve the hot soup with a sprinkle of chives over the top.

You've Got Skills

FLIPPING FOODS WITH A SPATULA

In order to make some of our favorite foods such as pancakes, grilled cheese sandwiches and quesadillas, it is important to know how to flip food with a spatula. It can be a little tricky at first—try not to get frustrated. With a little bit of practice, you'll be an expert flipper in no time.

The easiest spatula for kids to use is a wide slotted one made of flexible nylon or silicone. These bendy spatulas won't scratch your nonstick pans or griddles, and they are easier to maneuver underneath delicate foods like pancakes and eggs.

The key is to have patience and not flip your food too early or too often. Your goal is to cook the first side completely and only flip your food one time to cook the other side. Usually foods requiring a spatula are trying to get a golden toasty brown on each side. If you keep flipping, you won't get that toasted look.

NOTE: Flat items such as pancakes are easiest to flip. With a food that has layers like a sandwich or quesadilla, you might find it easier to have your adult helper hold your skillet stable while you use a long-handled spoon or tongs to hold the layers together while flipping them over.

1. **Get your skillet ready.** Preheat the skillet to the temperature the recipe recommends. You want it nice and hot before you add your main food. Add the cooking oil, butter, or cooking spray to the skillet, and let it heat through for a minute.

2. **Add your food to the skillet.** Carefully add your main food to the skillet. Once you place it in the pan, do not move it or rush to peek. You want the first side to get golden brown and cooked before flipping.

3. **Take a quick peek.** After at least 1 minute, carefully lift one corner of your food with the spatula so you can peek underneath. Does the first side look finished? Then it is ready to flip. If it still looks underdone, let it rest another minute before peeking again.

4. **Ready to flip!** When you're ready to flip your food over, hold your spatula in one hand and the handle of the skillet in your other hand. You don't want the skillet to wiggle away from you while you try to lift your food. Firmly slide the spatula as far under your food as you can get it. Lift your spatula up and quickly flip the food over on to the other side.

5. **Cook the other side.** Allow the food to fry on this side for a couple of minutes and get your plate ready near the stove. You can peek by lifting one corner of the food with the spatula to see if it's ready. You are looking for a wonderful golden brown color. When it looks finished, slide the spatula under the food and firmly grip the handle. Carefully lift up the food and bring it to your plate.

GRILLED HARVEST HAM & CHEESE SANDWICHES

Once you know how to make a classic grilled cheese sandwich, you have the perfect skills to make an easy dinner all year round. Change the fillings and it is a whole new meal! The best part? Everyone in the family can have it just the way they like it. Here we start with a kicked up version with savory ham and sweet apple, but you can use the same method with just plain cheese.

PLAY WITH IT! Next time try one of these combinations: A) turkey + cheddar cheese + thinly sliced fresh tomatoes; B) pepperoni + mozzarella cheese + sprinkle of basil; C) roast beef + Swiss cheese + thin spread of horseradish on the inside of the bread.

YIELD: 1 SANDWICH

1 green apple

2 slices of bread per sandwich

2 slices of Havarti cheese per sandwich

2 slices of thinly cut deli ham per sandwich

Butter, at room temperature for spreading plus more for the pan

1. HEY KIDS, PLEASE GET US STARTED!

Ask your adult helper to slice the green apple into thin pieces. It's okay to leave the skin on!

Line up one piece of bread for each sandwich on your cutting board. Top each slice with 1 piece of cheese, 1 slice of ham, and 2 to 3 thin slices of apple. Add the second slice of cheese on top of the apples, and then place the second slice of bread on top to form a sandwich. With a slice of cheese next to each slice of bread inside the sandwich, they will melt and hold everything together like glue!

Use a butter knife to spread a thin even layer of butter on the outside of both sides of each sandwich.

2. PARENTS, IT'S YOUR TURN!

Heat a skillet over medium heat.

3. TEAMWORK GETS IT DONE!

Place a small pat of butter into the skillet. Once it has melted, add your sandwich to the pan. Cook the sandwich for 3 to 4 minutes, and then flip it over carefully using a spatula. You may want to use a fork or butter knife to hold down the top slice of bread as you flip the sandwich over so that the fillings don't fall apart. Continue to cook for another 3 to 4 minutes until both sides are crispy and golden brown.

CHEESY CHICKEN QUESADILLAS

These cheesy pockets of happiness are the perfect place to use up the leftovers in your fridge for a simple lunch or dinner. We love to make them in an assembly line, and keep them toasty warm on a cookie sheet inside the oven so we can serve them family-style.

PLAY WITH IT! Taco flavor is the more traditional quesadilla method, but you could turn these into BBQ pork pockets with cheddar and shredded pork. How about ham and Swiss triangles using leftover deli meat, dipped into honey mustard? The trick is to make sure everything in your filling is cut up into small diced pieces so that the cheese can melt and work like glue to hold it all together.

YIELD: 4 SERVINGS

2 green onions

1 cup (230 g) shredded rotisserie chicken

8 medium-size tortillas

1–2 cups (111–222 g) shredded Colby Jack cheese

1 (16-oz [454-g]) jar prepared salsa, for serving

Sour cream, for serving

1. HEY KIDS, PLEASE GET US STARTED! ➤━━➤

Chop up the green onions with a butter knife, and place them in a small bowl by the stove.

Prepare the chicken by cutting it up with your butter knife or ripping it using your fingers. Place it in a small bowl by the stove.

Place the tortillas on a plate next to the stove.

Place the shredded cheese in a bowl, and set it by the stove.

Put a spoon inside the jar of salsa and another inside the container of sour cream, and place them on the table for serving.

2. PARENTS, ◀━━ IT'S YOUR TURN!

Place a medium-size skillet over medium-high heat.

OPTIONAL: If you want to serve the quesadillas family-style, preheat the oven to 225°F (110°C, or gas mark ¼), and place a cookie sheet inside.

3. TEAMWORK GETS IT DONE!

Spray the skillet with cooking spray, and place one tortilla flat on the pan.

Sprinkle 2 to 3 tablespoons (14 to 21 g) of shredded cheese over the whole tortilla face.

Sprinkle 2 tablespoons (29 g) of shredded chicken and 1 tablespoon (3 g) of green onions on one half of the tortilla face.

When the cheese has started to melt, use a spatula to flip the plain side of the tortilla (with just cheese, not the chicken side) over on top of the chicken side. The tortilla will now look like a half-moon with the melty cheese and chicken tucked inside.

Press down on the tortilla with the back of the spatula to glue all the melted cheese to the fillings. Transfer the quesadilla to a plate, and use a pizza cutter to slice it into 3 triangles. Serve with salsa and sour cream for dipping.

Repeat with remaining tortillas and filling.

To serve family-style: Store all the half-moon quesadillas on the cookie sheet in the warm oven until you've finished toasting up the entire batch. Use the pizza cutter to cut them into triangles, and serve on a platter for the whole family.

ZIPPY FRENCH DIP SANDWICHES

These sandwiches were built for dipping! Don't forget to serve a small cup of the broth on each plate so you can dunk them. We think the Montreal steak seasoning is worth buying; it's the secret ingredient in our hamburgers every summer. If you don't have it, you can substitute with a little sprinkle each of garlic salt, black pepper, crushed red pepper flakes and thyme.

PLAY WITH IT! You can add sliced peppers to the onion mix to make this a heartier sandwich. How about swapping the flavor of the cheese on the end? Or you can mix 1 to 2 tablespoons (15 to 30 g) of prepared horseradish sauce with 1 to 2 tablespoons (15 to 30 ml) of sour cream and spread a thin layer of it on the rolls before you fill them with the roast beef, if you'd like more flavor.

YIELD: 4 SERVINGS

½ small onion

1½ lb (680 g) deli sliced roast beef

2 tbsp (29 g) butter

1 tbsp (6 g) all-purpose flour

2 (14.5-oz [412-ml]) cans of beef broth

1 tbsp (15 ml) Worcestershire sauce

1 tbsp (15 g) Montreal Steak Seasoning

4 long sandwich rolls

4 slices Swiss cheese

1. HEY KIDS, PLEASE GET US STARTED! ➤➤➤

Ask your adult helper to cut the onion into quarters so you can chop it into small pieces using a manual food processor.

Cut the roast beef into 2-inch (5-cm) wide strips using a butter knife.

2. PARENTS, ←━━ IT'S YOUR TURN!

Place a large skillet over medium-high heat. Preheat the broiler in your oven.

3. TEAMWORK GETS IT DONE!

Measure the butter, and add it to the skillet to melt. Add the chopped onions and sauté them until softened, about 3 to 4 minutes. Measure and whisk in the flour, and toast it in the skillet for 1 minute.

Open the cans of beef broth and drizzle the broth into the skillet. Whisk it in with the flour and onions until smooth. Measure and add the Worcestershire sauce, giving the broth a quick stir to combine. Reduce the heat to medium-low.

Place the roast beef in the skillet and sprinkle it with the Montreal steak seasoning. Use a pair of tongs to gently toss and coat the meat in the beef broth.

As the beef warms through, place the sandwich rolls open face on a cookie sheet. The adult helper can toast them under the broiler for 1 minute. Watch carefully, they'll burn quickly!

Pile the hot beef inside each sandwich roll, and top with a slice of cheese. If you enjoy your cheese really melty, have your adult helper pop it back under the broiler for just a few seconds. Serve with a dipping cup of the broth from the pan.

SHREDDED HOT ITALIAN BEEF SANDWICHES

These spicy beef sandwiches are popular with Dad who loads them up with jarred peppers, but the kids gobble them up with just the melty cheese. We love to serve them on football Sundays in the fall. Serve them with salty potato chips and fresh veggies and dip for a simple meal.

PLAY WITH IT! You can change the seasoning mix to be less spicy: ranch or French onion soup mix seasonings work well, too! You can also add more veggies to the pot as it cooks: sliced onions or peppers work great.

YIELD: 8 TO 10 SERVINGS

FOR THE MEAT FILLING

3 cups (710 ml) beef broth

1 tsp salt

1 tsp pepper

1 tsp dried oregano

1 tsp dried basil

1 tsp dried parsley

1 tsp garlic powder

1 bay leaf

1 (0.7-oz [20-g]) package of dry Zesty Italian–style salad dressing mix

1 (5-lb [2.3 kg]) rump roast

FOR THE SANDWICHES

Crusty rolls

Pepper Jack or Swiss cheese

Jarred sliced peppers (such as jalapeños or red peppers)

1. HEY KIDS, PLEASE GET US STARTED! ➤➤⟶

Measure the beef broth, and pour it into the bowl of a slow cooker. Measure and add the salt, pepper, oregano, basil, parsley and garlic powder. Add the bay leaf to the pot. Stir in the packet of salad dressing seasonings.

2. PARENTS, ⟵⟵ IT'S YOUR TURN!

Help rinse the rump roast and pat it dry with paper towels. Gently place the roast into the slow cooker, and turn it to coat in the seasonings.

Cover the slow cooker with its lid, and cook on low for 10 to 12 hours or on high for 4 to 5 hours.

3. TEAMWORK GETS IT DONE!

When the beef is finished cooking, use 2 forks to shred the meat inside the crockpot. It will be very tender and should practically fall apart when you poke it.

Slice the rolls and open them flat. Lay them on a cookie sheet and have the adult helper lightly toast them under the oven broiler for 1 to 2 minutes. Watch them carefully, they'll burn quickly!

Serve the beef piled up on your lightly toasted rolls with layers of cheese and spicy peppers.

CAJUN ROLL-UP FINGERTIP SANDWICHES

These spicy little sandwich rolls are perfect for dunking into soup. We love to match them with the Confetti Veggie Soup (page 56) to tame the spice a little. You could always swap up the fillings to make a sandwich that isn't spicy at all!

PLAY WITH IT! Any deli meat and cheese combo you love would work great here. Some yummy veggies that work well mixed in are broccoli, green onions or diced peppers. You could even do a Hawaiian version with ham, Swiss, green onions and diced fresh pineapple!

YIELD: 4 TO 6 SERVINGS

1 medium tomato

1 (11-oz [311-g]) package of refrigerated French bread dough. (You can find this near the refrigerated biscuits and cinnamon rolls at your grocery store.)

½ lb (227 g) sliced deli turkey. (We prefer a spicy Cajun flavored variety.)

1 cup (121 g) shredded cheddar cheese

1. HEY KIDS, PLEASE GET US STARTED!

Have your helper cut the tomato into quarters. Then, over the sink use your fingers to separate the watery part with the seeds from the solid part of the tomato. You don't want the seeds to make your sandwich soggy! Take the solid part of the tomato and chop it into small pieces with a manual food processor.

Lay out a large cookie sheet. Open the package of dough along the seam, and roll out the bread to form a flat square.

Lay the deli turkey slices out over the surface of the dough in a single layer.

Measure out and sprinkle the shredded cheese over the surface of the turkey. Sprinkle the tomato pieces evenly over the top of the cheese.

Starting from the long edge of the dough, roll the turkey and cheese up into the dough like a long pinwheel. Place it on the cookie sheet so that the open seam is face down on the pan.

Use your butter knife to slice 4 short angled cuts along on the top of the dough to let steam escape from the fillings.

2. PARENTS, IT'S YOUR TURN!

While your kid chef is preparing the sandwiches, preheat the oven to 350°F (175°C, or gas mark 4).

3. TEAMWORK GETS IT DONE!

Bake the bread for 20 minutes or until the top is golden brown and crispy.

Slice the sandwich into 1- to 2-inch (2.5- to 5-cm) wide slices, and serve.

EASY PEASY DINNERS

Now we're ready to prepare the main meal of the day. Who's hungry for dinner? Once you have a few basic skills for cooking several kinds of meat, you'll be ready to really play in the kitchen.

Simply change the seasonings and veggies in any of these recipes and you'll have a completely new dish that you've invented yourself. From super fast dinners like School Night Chicken Fajitas (page 84) to slower favorites like Grandma's Classic Roast Chicken (page 96) there is sure to be a recipe that fits your pocket of time. Don't miss the Mustard Glazed Salmon with Asparagus (page 104) and the Sweet-and-Spicy Pork Tenderloin with Roasted Carrots (page 98) when you are eager to try out some new cooking skills.

In this chapter, you'll be using your hands to prepare several different kinds of meat. You can control your hands better than any other tool in the kitchen, and they work best for preparing some of these dishes. If the idea of handling raw meat makes you uncomfortable, stock disposable cooking gloves in your kitchen. Be sure to find the non-powdered variety, and only use them to prepare one meal before disposing.

You've Got Skills

HOW TO BROIL CHICKEN TENDERLOINS

Broiling chicken tenderloins is one of the quickest and easiest ways to prepare chicken. It's a little like grilling your food, but much easier and happens all inside your kitchen. Chicken tenderloins work better than other chicken pieces because they are thinner, smaller portions of meat that cook through evenly before burning on the outside the way a thicker piece of meat would.

To broil your chicken, you need three important things: a prepared broiling pan, a marinade or seasoning blend and a meat thermometer. A broiler pan is a two-piece pan that has a top piece with slits in it for draining. Line the bottom piece with tin foil to catch the juices that will drip down from your meat and veggies for easy clean-up. If you don't have one, you might be able to substitute a rimmed baking sheet, but check with your adult helper to make sure it is safe for using with the high temperatures of the broiler.

A marinade is a mixture of seasonings and oil that soaks into your meat and makes it more tender and juicy. You'll find recipes for our 3 favorite blends on the next page.

To use the meat thermometer to test the temperature at the end, put the tip in the center of the thickest part of the chicken tenderloin. That is the spot that needs the most time to cook all the way through. Leave the tip in place until the temperature display stops changing.

Now let's test your broiling skills!

CHICKEN MARINADE, THREE WAYS

These simple marinade recipes are a perfect way to make an easy chicken dinner. Spice up and broil some chicken ahead of time and you can chop the cooked tenderloins to include in a sandwich wrap or on top of a salad in a pinch.

YIELD: 4 TO 6 SERVINGS

GREEK VINAIGRETTE

1½ tsp (1 g) oregano

1 tsp thyme

½ tsp basil

½ tsp marjoram

½ tsp minced onion

¼ tsp garlic

1 tbsp (15 ml) red wine vinegar

2 tbsp (30 ml) olive oil

HONEY SOY GINGER

2 tbsp (30 ml) honey

3 tbsp (44 ml) soy sauce

2 tbsp (30 ml) olive oil

2 tsp (6 g) jarred minced garlic

½ tsp dried ginger

Sprinkle of red pepper flakes

BBQ SEASONED

2 tsp (9 g) packed brown sugar

1 tsp paprika

Salt & pepper

1 tsp chili powder

½ tsp garlic powder

¼ tsp nutmeg

¼ tsp cayenne pepper

3 tbsp (45 ml) olive oil

1–2 lbs (453–907 g) chicken tenderloins

1. HEY KIDS, PLEASE GET US STARTED! ➤——→

Choose which marinade you want to try. Combine the ingredients in a measuring cup, and stir together with a fork. Add 1 to 2 pounds (453 to 907 g) of chicken tenderloins to a plastic zip top baggie. Pour the marinade in, and close and seal the bag. Toss the bag gently to coat the chicken in the marinade until all the pieces are nicely coated.

2. PARENTS, ←——◄ IT'S YOUR TURN!

Set the top rack of your oven to a position so that the top of the broiling pan is 4 to 6 inches (10 to 15 cm) away from the broiler. Preheat the broiler in your oven.

3. TEAMWORK GETS IT DONE!

Use a fork or tongs to remove the chicken from the marinade, and place the pieces on the top tray of the broiler pan over the sections that have the open slits. Leave space between each piece so they cook evenly.

Place the pan under the broiler and cook for 7 minutes. Remove the pan from the oven, turn the chicken over and then cook for an additional 5 minutes. The chicken will be slightly charred and should be a minimum of 180°F (82°C) internal temperature. Be sure to check carefully with a food thermometer.

SCHOOL NIGHT CHICKEN FAJITAS

No need to wait for Taco Tuesday to enjoy these chicken fajitas, they are so easy to make. You could even do big batches of chicken over the weekend and use the leftovers to pack yummy lunches for school. My girls love them hot or cold.

PLAY WITH IT! Fajitas are always a favorite because everyone can mix and match their very favorite toppings. Try setting out any combination you like: corn, fresh tomatoes, chopped green onions, beans, prepared salsa, fresh cilantro, lime wedges or sour cream.

YIELD: 4 TO 6 SERVINGS

1 tbsp (8 g) chili powder

1¼ tsp (3 g) cumin

¾ tsp paprika

¾ tsp oregano

¾ tsp marjoram

¾ tsp thyme

¾ tsp garlic salt

½ tsp basil

½ tsp cayenne pepper

½ tsp nutmeg

Juice from 1 lime

3 tbsp (45 ml) canola oil

2 lb (907 g) chicken tenderloins

1 red bell pepper

½ red onion

8 small flour tortillas

1. HEY KIDS, PLEASE GET US STARTED!

Measure all the seasonings, and stir them together in a small bowl. This makes a large batch of fajita seasoning. You will use 1 tablespoon (8 g) for every 2 pounds (907 g) of chicken. Save the remaining mix in an airtight container so your seasoning will be all ready to go next time you want to make this dish.

Wash the lime, and then cut it in half and squeeze the juice into a measuring cup. Measure and add the canola oil, and stir it together with the juice. Add 1 tablespoon (8 g) of your seasoning blend to the cup and stir.

Place the chicken tenderloins in a large zip top plastic bag. Pour in the spice-juice-oil mixture and seal the bag shut. Gently toss the chicken in the marinade until all the pieces are coated with the oil and spices.

2. PARENTS, IT'S YOUR TURN!

Slice the pepper and onions into thin strips. Add them to the bag of chicken pieces, seal the bag and gently toss.

Preheat the broiler in your oven. Line a broiling pan with tin foil.

3. TEAMWORK GETS IT DONE!

Use a fork or tongs to separate the chicken from the peppers, and place just the chicken on your prepared broiling pan. Broil for 7 minutes.

Flip the chicken pieces over so both sides brown. Pour the reserved peppers and onions down the middle of the broiling pan, and return the pan to the oven. Broil for 5 more minutes.

The chicken should be cooked through, and the peppers and onions should be tender and beginning to char. If the veggies need another minute, remove the chicken to a cutting board before putting the peppers back under the broiler. Slice the chicken into smaller pieces while the peppers finish in the oven.

Place the tortillas on a microwave-safe plate, cover them with a dampened paper towel and heat for 20 to 30 seconds on high.

Serve the chicken and peppers in a large bowl, and let everyone top their fajitas with their favorite items.

You've Got Skills

HOW TO BROWN GROUND BEEF

One of the easiest cuts of meat to cook for beginners is ground beef—or ground pork, ground turkey or ground chicken. You get the idea! You simply need one skillet, one spoon and no knives.

You can make countless dishes in a wide variety of flavors from savory Italian spaghetti sauce (page 132) to spicy Potsticker Stir-Fry (page 164). But it's quite possible that everyone's favorite ground beef recipe is tacos! Use the awesome taco recipe on the next page to practice browning ground beef. All you need to get started is a large sauté pan and a long-handled spoon. Our favorite tool has a pinwheel shaped edge that easily chops the meat into small pieces, but any long-handled kitchen spoon will do.

NOT JUST FOR TUESDAY TACOS

This might be one of the easiest dinner recipes to launch your cooking adventures. Preparing the filling is easy, deciding what to put on your taco is where the real hard work begins. If you are interested in mixing up your own custom batch of taco seasoning, we've included a tasty recipe below. Feel free to substitute with a packet of seasoning from the store. The benefit to making your own is you can make it as spicy or not spicy as you like. Our seasoning recipe makes more than you'll need, so keep the extras in the pantry for quick taco dinners any night of the week!

PLAY WITH IT! Your topping choices are practically endless. Try adding fresh tomatoes, corn, chopped green onions, lettuce, red onion, bell peppers or beans. You could also use the filling to make a simple taco salad using lettuce and tortilla strips, topped with sour cream and salsa for dressing.

YIELD: 4 TO 6 SERVINGS

HOMEMADE TACO SEASONING
¼ cup (30 g) chili powder

3 tbsp (23 g) cumin

2 tbsp (12 g) all-purpose flour

1 tbsp (7 g) paprika

1 tbsp (7 g) crushed red pepper

1 tbsp (15 g) salt

2 tsp (5 g) unsweetened cocoa powder

1½ tsp (4 g) garlic powder

1½ tsp (4 g) onion powder

1½ tsp (1 g) oregano

1½ tsp (3 g) allspice

1½ tsp (8 g) black pepper

TACOS
1 lb (454 g) ground beef

½ cup (118 ml) water

Tortillas, soft shell or crunchy (your choice!)

Your choice of taco toppings

1. HEY KIDS, PLEASE GET US STARTED!

Measure and mix a batch of taco seasoning blend. Measure out 4 tablespoons (60 g) of the blend for the batch of tacos, and set it aside next to the stove. You can store the extra seasoning in your pantry in a tightly sealed container. Next time you're making tacos, remember to use 4 tablespoons (60 g) of the blend per 1 pound (454 g) of ground meat. This recipe makes enough seasoning for 4 batches of tacos.

Have your helper place a large skillet over medium-high heat. Add the ground beef, and cook it until it is no longer pink. Use a long-handled spoon to break it up into smaller pieces as it cooks. This will help it cook evenly and thoroughly.

2. PARENTS, IT'S YOUR TURN!

Once the beef is cooked through, drain excess fat from the pan and return it to medium heat.

3. TEAMWORK GETS IT DONE!

Add the reserved 4 tablespoons (60 g) of taco seasoning blend to the beef. Stir it together and toast the seasonings for 1 minute. Pour in the water and stir. The spices will form a slightly thickened sauce.

Heat your tortillas according to the directions on the package, and serve them alongside the taco filling.

BIG BATCH PORK PICADILLO

Now that you are a Taco Master, it's time to graduate to the next step: spicy pork picadillo. This sweet and spicy Cuban dish is perfect for burrito bowls or nachos. Kids, how many juicy raisins will you find hidden in the seasoned pork? Parents, you'll love that this recipe makes a very large batch so that you can cook once and freeze the leftovers in smaller portions.

PLAY WITH IT! The picadillo is delicious by itself, or you could use it to make homemade nachos with melted cheese and fresh tomatoes.

NOTE: This recipe calls for chipotle in adobo, a canned good you can find at your grocery store in the Mexican food section. Freeze any extras for future use, so the peppers don't go to waste.

YIELD: 10 TO 12 SERVINGS

¾ tsp chili powder

½ tsp cinnamon

¼ tsp cumin

¼ tsp cloves

Sprinkle of salt & pepper

½ cup (76 g) raisins

1 small onion

1 chipotle pepper from a (7-oz [198-g]) can of chipotle peppers in adobo sauce

1 (28-oz [794-g]) can whole tomatoes in puree

1 tbsp (15 ml) olive oil

2 tsp (7 g) jarred minced garlic

1 (6-oz [170-g]) can of tomato paste

3 lb (1.4 kg) ground pork

2 tbsp (30 ml) apple cider vinegar

1 bay leaf

1. HEY KIDS, PLEASE GET US STARTED! ➤➤➤

Measure the chili powder, cinnamon, cumin, cloves, salt and pepper, and stir them together in a small bowl. Set it aside.

Measure the raisins and put them in a bowl.

Chop up the onion in a manual food processor until the pieces are all about the same size. Put them in a bowl.

Chop up the chipotle pepper in a manual food processor until the pieces are itty bitty.

Use a can opener to open the tomatoes. Then use kitchen scissors to cut the tomatoes up right inside of their can!

2. PARENTS, IT'S YOUR TURN! ◄◄

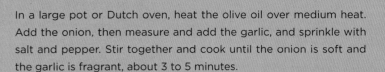

In a large pot or Dutch oven, heat the olive oil over medium heat. Add the onion, then measure and add the garlic, and sprinkle with salt and pepper. Stir together and cook until the onion is soft and the garlic is fragrant, about 3 to 5 minutes.

Add the tomato paste, the chopped chipotle pepper and the dried seasonings to the pot. Stir to combine with the onions and the garlic, and heat for 1 minute until fragrant.

3. TEAMWORK GETS IT DONE!

Add the ground pork to the pot and let the kids use a long-handled spoon to break it up as it browns. Make sure to stir it in with the seasoned onion mixture as it cooks. As the pork adds juices to the pot, use the back of your spoon to scrape up any dried bits of seasoning on the bottom. Cook until the pork is no longer pink, about 10 to 12 minutes.

Kids can then add the tomatoes in their puree and the cider vinegar to the pot. Stir to combine. Add the bay leaf to the mixture, and bring everything to a boil. Reduce the heat to keep the mixture at a simmer. Cook partially covered until thickened, 35 to 40 minutes total.

Kids can now toss the raisins into the pot, and stir to combine. Look for and remove the bay leaf as you stir. The heat and moisture from the dish will partially rehydrate the raisins and warm them through.

To freeze: Cool the picadillo to room temperature. Divide the mix among several airtight containers in 1- to 2-cup (245- to 490-g) portions for easy thawing. Label the containers with the date you prepared it and freeze them up to 3 months.

You've Got Skills

COOKING A LARGE CUT OF MEAT

While smaller cuts of meat cook quickly and are easy to prepare, larger cuts of meat such as pork tenderloins, whole chickens and beef roasts are delicious ways to feed your family. If you try to sauté or broil a large cut of meat, the outside would burn before the center was cooked to a safe temperature. By cooking the meat low and slow, you reduce your cooking temperature and cook the meat for a much longer period of time so that the center has a chance to catch up to the outside. This method will give you tender, juicy meat.

We have three favorite tools for cooking a roast. The first is a roasting pan—a large deep pan that will hold all the juices from the meat along with veggies at the bottom without spilling over. In a pinch, a 9 x 13-inch (23 x 33-cm) glass baking dish can often be used instead. The second is a Dutch oven, which is a heavy-duty pot with a lid that traps the heat inside. You can brown meats on the stove top before placing the pot in the oven to finish cooking. Our third favorite is a slow cooker: a countertop appliance that plugs in and works electronically. The heat level options are usually just Low or High. Slow cooker recipes tend to take anywhere from 3 to 8 hours so they are great options for weekends. You can also use baking sheets, ovenproof skillets or an Instant Pot® to cook your roast. Don't be afraid to swap the cooking tool we recommend with something else you have on hand that might work.

Use the recipe for the sweet-and-spicy pork on the next page to practice cooking a large pork roast in either a Dutch oven or slow cooker.

SWEET-AND-SPICY SHREDDED PORK

Shredded pork for sandwiches is the perfect place to start when you are cooking your first large roast. It's almost impossible to mess up because the entire point is to cook it until it actually falls apart all by itself!

YIELD: 8 TO 12 SERVINGS

1 onion

1 tsp dried oregano

1 tsp cumin

1 tsp chili powder

½ tsp paprika

1 tbsp (15 g) salt

3 tsp (30 g) jarred minced garlic

1 tbsp (15 ml) olive oil

2 tbsp (30 ml) white wine vinegar

¼ cup (55 g) packed brown sugar

1 (4–6 lb [1.8–2.7 kg]) pork shoulder (Also known as pork butt, but we promise that's just a funny name!)

2 cups (473 ml) water

1–2 (18-oz [492-ml]) jars barbecue sauce, for serving

1. HEY KIDS, PLEASE GET US STARTED! ➤➤→

Have your helper cut the onion into quarters so you can chop it up into small pieces with a manual food processor. Transfer the onions to a small mixing bowl.

Measure and add the oregano, cumin, chili powder, paprika, salt, garlic, oil, vinegar and brown sugar to the mixing bowl. Stir it all together with the onions.

Place the pork roast in your sink and remove all the outer packaging. Rinse the pork roast under cold water. Pat it dry with paper towels and throw them out immediately after.

Place the pork inside a slow cooker or Dutch oven. Pour the onion mixture over the top, and rub it all over with the back of a spoon. Pour the water into the pot, and cover it with a lid.

2. PARENTS, ➤➤→ IT'S YOUR TURN!

If using a Dutch oven, preheat the oven to 300°F (150°C, or gas mark 2).

3. TEAMWORK GETS IT DONE!

If using a Dutch oven, cook the roast for 4 to 5 hours depending on its weight. A rough estimate is to plan for 45 minutes per pound (454 g) but no less than 4 hours. Set a timer for every hour, and take the pot out of the oven so you can check and turn the pork over. This allows for it to develop crispy bits on both sides.

If using a slow cooker, cook the roast for 5 to 7 hours on high or 9 to 11 hours on low. No turning necessary.

When the pork has finished cooking, it should be fall-apart tender. Let it rest for 10 minutes and then use a slotted spoon to remove the pork to a large serving bowl. Use 2 forks to shred the meat. If the meat appears too dry, spoon some of the juices from the pan over the meat and toss to combine.

Serve the meat either plain or with a drizzle of barbecue sauce over the top.

GRANDMA'S CLASSIC ROAST CHICKEN

Do you know I was too scared to cook a whole chicken until I was so old I already had two kids of my own? Once you've roasted a chicken, you'll realize just how easy it actually is. Just imagine grandma's face when you walk to the table with a chicken you made yourself! Few dishes will make you feel as grown-up as this one.

PLAY WITH IT! You could swap up the herbs you put inside the chicken and try rosemary or sage instead of the thyme. You can also add different veggies or even add fruit to the pan. Try parsnips, apples, butternut squash or sweet potatoes. Just remember to chop them up evenly!

YIELD: 4 TO 6 SERVINGS

2 tbsp (28 g) butter

1 whole roasting chicken, about 4 lbs (1.8 kg)

1 lemon

1 small bunch of fresh thyme

1 small onion

3 carrots

6 baby red potatoes

1 tbsp (15 ml) olive oil

Sprinkle of salt & pepper

1. HEY KIDS, PLEASE GET US STARTED!

Measure and place the butter in a microwave-safe container, and melt it on high for 20 seconds. Set it by your work space for later.

Place the chicken in your kitchen sink and get a few paper towels handy right next to your work space. Use kitchen scissors to unwrap the outer packaging materials from the chicken and throw them away. Rinse the chicken with cold water on both the inside and the outside. Pat the chicken dry on the outside with the paper towels and then throw them away.

Place the clean, dry chicken on a large plate.

Wash the lemon and then use a fork to prick small holes all over its surface. Place the lemon inside of the hole of the chicken.

Rinse and dry the fresh thyme and place the sprigs inside the chicken, too. Stems and everything.

Paint the cooled, melted butter over the top of the chicken with a pastry brush. Pay special attention to the legs and get the butter all over the top.

2. PARENTS, IT'S YOUR TURN!

Cut the onion, carrots and potatoes into large chunks, and place them inside the bottom of a roasting pan. Have your kid chef toss the veggies with the olive oil until coated, and then sprinkle them with salt and pepper.

Preheat the oven to 425°F (220°C, or gas mark 7). Place the pan of veggies in the oven for 15 minutes.

3. TEAMWORK GETS IT DONE!

Remove the veggies from the oven and give them a toss with a large spoon. Carefully, place the chicken on the bed of vegetables. Parents, you might want to do this so your child doesn't get burned by the hot pan.

Return the chicken pan to the oven and roast for 18 to 20 minutes per pound (454 g), or until the thigh meat reaches a minimum of 180°F (82°C). Use your food thermometer to check.

The bird will be golden brown with crispy skin. Let it rest for 10 minutes before your adult helper carves it. You can carve the chicken however you prefer, but we like to slice it down the middle, remove each breast and then cut the breast meat into slices. The legs should easily lift away with a gentle cut at the base.

To serve your dish to the family, place the roasted veggies on one side of a large platter and add the sliced chicken on the other side.

SWEET-AND-SPICY PORK WITH ROASTED CARROTS

Pork tenderloins are perfect for busy weeknight dinners. They cook a lot more quickly than larger roasts and are so tender. Roasting them on a cookie sheet with some veggies means that the sweet glaze from the meat will melt all over the carrots and make everything taste extra delicious.

PLAY WITH IT! Because the pork only cooks for 30 minutes, we chose simple veggies that can also roast quickly. You could use potatoes or sweet potatoes if you cut them up extra small. Peppers, onions, zucchini or even cherry tomatoes and asparagus would also taste delicious here, but are very delicate. Add them to the pan when the pork is halfway done cooking so they don't burn.

YIELD: 6 TO 8 SERVINGS

5 large carrots

1 tbsp (15 ml) olive oil

¼ tsp dried ginger

2 tsp (10 g) kosher salt

1 tsp cumin

1 tsp chili powder

1 tsp cinnamon

½ tsp dried thyme

½ tsp pepper

2 pork tenderloins

2 tbsp (30 ml) olive oil

⅓ cup (74 g) packed brown sugar

2 tsp (7 g) jarred minced garlic

1 tsp hot sauce, such as Tabasco

1. HEY KIDS, PLEASE GET US STARTED!

Wash and peel the carrots, then pass them along to your helper to cut into thick slices on an angle.

Add the carrot slices to a small mixing bowl or zip top baggie. Toss them with 1 tablespoon (15 ml) of olive oil and the dried ginger. Lay them in a single layer on a baking sheet. Sprinkle them with salt and pepper.

Measure the salt, cumin, chili powder, cinnamon, thyme and pepper, and stir them together in a small bowl.

Place the pork tenderloins on the baking sheet. Sprinkle the seasoning blend over the top of both of them, and rub it in all over the surface. Wash your hands.

Measure the 2 tablespoons (30 ml) of olive oil, brown sugar, garlic and hot sauce, and stir them together in the same bowl you used for the seasoning mix. Pour this over the top of the pork tenderloins and spread it evenly.

2. PARENTS, IT'S YOUR TURN!

When your kid chef asks, trim the ends of the carrots and then slice them into thick chunks at an angle. Then pass them back for finishing.

Preheat the oven to 375°F (190°C, or gas mark 5).

3. TEAMWORK GETS IT DONE!

Roast the pork tenderloin and carrots for 30 minutes or until the pork is 150°F (65°C) at the center. Remove from the oven and cover the pan loosely with tinfoil. Let the meat rest for 10 minutes before your adult helper slices it.

You've Got Skills
INTRODUCTION TO SEAFOOD

Do you enjoy eating at seafood restaurants? Have you ever tried to make fish right at home? It took us a long time to become brave enough to attempt it in our family. But once we did, there was no looking back!

Seafood is filled with something called omega-3 fatty acids that help boost your brainpower. Because we wanted to benefit from all those wonderful things fish can do for our bodies, we began planning "Fishy Fridays" every week. We experimented with tons of fish recipes to learn which we loved best.

Use the recipe on the next page to try cooking fish—it might become a favorite!

When you're first trying fish, start with something mild, white and flaky. Our favorites are cod, tilapia and halibut. They don't have a strong taste and will take on the flavor of whatever seasonings you use.

Be sure to give salmon a try next. It has a little stronger flavor but a wonderful texture. My youngest prefers to call it "pink fish"! The Mustard Glazed Salmon on page 104 is her favorite.

Once you're a fish pro, be sure to try the Roasted Shrimp with Garlic and Lemon on page 106. It's the perfect fancy meal to make for your family.

MAGIC CRUNCHY COATED FISH

Our favorite way to prepare fish or shellfish is to roast it in the oven with some veggies. You can mix up the seasonings to be as spicy as you like. If you are a fish newbie, adding some butter and crispy breadcrumbs is a perfect way to try it because it helps to mask the new texture with a familiar and delicious crunch.

PLAY WITH IT! Add any mixture of seasonings you love to the breadcrumbs: a pinch of cayenne to make it spicy, some lemon pepper to give it zing or single seasonings such as basil, dill, oregano or even a little grated Parmesan cheese are all delicious here.

YIELD: 4 SERVINGS

1½ cups (181 g) panko breadcrumbs

2 tsp (10 g) garlic salt

¼ tsp paprika

½ cup (115 ml) melted butter

4 fish filets: tilapia, flounder or cod

1 tbsp (15 ml) olive oil

1. HEY KIDS, PLEASE GET US STARTED!

Measure and mix the breadcrumbs and seasonings together in a small bowl. Place the butter in a microwave-safe container and heat it for 20 seconds, or until melted. Stir the butter into the breadcrumbs with a fork, and mix until all the crumbs are dampened.

Place the fish filets on a baking sheet. Brush their tops with the olive oil. Gently press the breadcrumbs evenly over the top of each filet.

2. PARENTS, IT'S YOUR TURN!

Preheat the oven to 375°F (190°C, or gas mark 5).

3. TEAMWORK GETS IT DONE!

Bake the fish for 12 to 15 minutes, or until the fish flakes easily with a fork.

MUSTARD-GLAZED SALMON WITH ASPARAGUS

In our family, "pink fish" is a special treat. It's one of my kids' favorite foods! Our favorite seasoning blend has whole mustard seeds mixed in that give it a fun texture, but if you don't like the crunch feel free to substitute just regular Dijon mustard instead. The brown sugar helps form a delicious crunchy coating on the outside of the fish.

PLAY WITH IT! You can season the salmon with any seasoning blend you prefer. Make it as spicy, or not, as you like. Because it cooks so quickly, stick to delicate vegetables if you want to play with the asparagus mix. Cherry tomatoes, pea pods, zucchini or broccoli would be delicious.

YIELD: 4 TO 6 SERVINGS

4–6 salmon filets, skins removed

1 tsp onion powder

1 tsp pepper

1 tsp salt

1 tsp thyme

2 tsp (5 g) paprika

¼ tsp sage

¼ tsp rosemary

½ tsp chili powder

1 tbsp (14 g) packed brown sugar

1 tsp dried mustard seeds

1 tbsp (14 g) butter

1 bunch of asparagus

1 tbsp (15 ml) olive oil

1. HEY KIDS, PLEASE GET US STARTED!

Place the salmon filets on a large baking sheet.

Measure the onion powder, pepper, salt, thyme, paprika, sage, rosemary, chili powder, brown sugar and mustard seeds, and mix them together in a small bowl.

Put the butter in a microwave-safe dish and heat it for 15 seconds, or until melted. Brush the butter over the tops of the salmon filets using a pastry brush, or drizzle and spread it out with the back of a spoon. Sprinkle the seasoning mix evenly over the top of the salmon.

Asparagus have tough ends. Take each stalk and gently bend it until the cut end snaps off. Throw away the tough ends and have your helper cut the remaining stalks into 2-inch (5-cm) pieces. Use a zip top baggie or small bowl to toss the asparagus with the olive oil, and then sprinkle them around the salmon on the baking sheet. Sprinkle them with a little bit of salt and pepper.

2. PARENTS, IT'S YOUR TURN!

Preheat the oven to 425°F (220°C, or gas mark 7).

When your kid chef asks, cut the asparagus into 2-inch (5-cm) pieces on an angle and then hand them back for finishing.

3. TEAMWORK GETS IT DONE!

Bake the salmon and asparagus for 15 to 20 minutes until the salmon easily flakes apart when you poke it with a fork.

ROASTED SHRIMP WITH GARLIC AND LEMON

Our grandpa nicknamed these "Peanuts of the Sea" because shrimp come in shells that need to be peeled before you eat them. To make this recipe easier for our busy schedule, we love to use already peeled and deveined shrimp. It's a perfect quick dish to make when you're in a rush, but fancy enough to serve to friends.

PLAY WITH IT! Lemon garlic seasoning goes so well with most seafood, but you could swap that for a hot Cajun blend, spicy taco blend or some Old Bay seasoning. Shrimp are a simple blank palette for whatever spices you love.

YIELD: 4 TO 6 SERVINGS

3 tsp (9 g) jarred minced garlic

2 tbsp (30 ml) olive oil

2 shakes of hot sauce, such as Tabasco

1 lemon

1 lb (454 g) peeled and deveined raw shrimp (thawed and drained if frozen)

2 tbsp (29 g) butter

1 bunch asparagus

1 cup (149 g) cherry tomatoes

1 tbsp (15 ml) olive oil

Salt & pepper

Fresh bread or prepared pasta, for serving (optional)

1. HEY KIDS, PLEASE GET US STARTED! →

Measure the garlic, 2 tablespoons (30 ml) of olive oil and hot sauce, and mix them together in a medium-size mixing bowl. Wash and cut the lemon in half and squeeze the juices in with the olive oil mixture. Stir them together.

Add the shrimp to the bowl and stir it together with the oil until everything is coated. Pour the shrimp out onto one side of a baking sheet, and spread them in a single layer. Be sure to scrape the bowl with a spatula and get all the oil mixture onto the shrimp.

Cut the butter into small chunks, and sprinkle it over the shrimp.

Asparagus have tough ends. Take each stalk and gently bend it until the cut end snaps off. Discard the tough ends and have your helper cut the remaining stalks into 2-inch (5-cm) pieces. Add the asparagus and cherry tomatoes to the mixing bowl, and toss them with 1 more tablespoon (15 ml) of olive oil. Place the veggies on the other half of the baking sheet.

Sprinkle the entire pan with a little salt and pepper.

2. PARENTS, ← IT'S YOUR TURN!

Preheat the oven to 400°F (200°C, or gas mark 6).

When your kid chef asks, cut the asparagus into 2-inch (5-cm) pieces on an angle and then hand them back for finishing.

3. TEAMWORK GETS IT DONE!

Roast the shrimp and veggies for 10 minutes. You know they are finished when the shrimp is nice and pink, curled up and firm.

OPTIONAL: There is plenty of butter sauce from this dish for you to serve the shrimp with bread for dipping or over your favorite pasta.

CLASSIC COMFORT FOODS ♥

A comfort food is a warm and cozy meal that reminds you of home and love. Even if some of these recipes are new to you, they'll likely make your family smile really big when you serve them.

Comfort foods fill your house with amazing smells and get everyone running to the dinner table. Which one will be your new favorite? We're guessing the Mini Meatball Skillet (page 120) with warm fresh bread for dunking! Or maybe it will be my older daughter's favorite rich and creamy Cozy Country Potato Pie (page 116) or my younger daughter's favorite lightened up Crustless Chicken Potpie (page 112). There are always cheers in our house when those recipes hit the menu list for the week.

You've Got Skills

HOW TO SAUTÉ VEGGIES

Cooking is like magic. We take a few ingredients that might seem icky all by themselves and turn them into something that smells amazing. I always giggled when my kids would tell me they didn't like onions or garlic because they are hiding in all of their very favorite foods! Pizza and tacos just wouldn't taste right if they didn't have onions and garlic somewhere inside. The trick is all in how you prepare it and the magic that happens in your skillet.

A raw onion is harsh and strong to taste. Garlic is super stinky when it is raw and fresh, and it doesn't smell like something you'd want to eat. However, when you melt some butter or olive oil in a skillet and cook the onion and garlic until it is clear and soft, they suddenly taste sweet. This process is called sautéing.

Cook the veggies until the onions are translucent (clear) and softened. If they are starting to turn black on the edges, your pan might be too hot or you've cooked them too long. Charred onions can still be delicious in some recipes, especially roasted dishes, but for most sautéed recipes you want to stop before that happens.

1. **Choose your cooking oil:** Canola oil, olive oil, butter or a combination will help coat the pan and keep the food from sticking. Oil also adds a nice flavor to your dish. The recipe will specify which one you need.

2. **Choose your pan:** Skillets come in many different sizes. For most recipes in this book, you'll need a large one that can fit your whole finished recipe. We prefer nonstick pans because you don't need as much oil to keep food from sticking. Just be careful you're using wood or silicone/nylon tools and not metal ones. Metal will scratch the coating.

3. **Chop your veggies:** You'll need to chop the veggies before you sauté them, and once they're cooked that's the size they'll be in your final recipe.

4. **Heat your oil or butter:** Place your skillet on a burner of the stove top, and then turn the heat for that burner on to medium. Add the oil or butter to the skillet, and give it 2 to 3 minutes to heat up before you add your veggies. Everyone's stove heats pans a little differently. To test if your skillet is ready, add one small piece of onion to the pan. If it sizzles, you're ready to go.

5. **Add the veggies to the pan:** Carefully pour the chopped veggies into your pan. Keep your hands away from the pan and use a spoon to scoop them out of the bowl or measuring cup they were waiting in so that the hot oil doesn't splatter on you.

6. **Sauté the veggies:** Stir the veggies around in the pan, and then let them rest and simmer. Every couple of minutes, you can give them another stir. By letting them sit in between your stirrings, you are allowing the veggies to develop a golden-brown color that makes them extra sweet and delicious.

CRUSTLESS CHICKEN POTPIE

Sometimes when we don't like a food, it's just one part of the food that is the problem. It turns out my kids love chicken potpie filling but they don't like the pie itself! That's an easy enough problem to fix, we just serve up the creamy chicken and veggies alongside our favorite biscuits instead. Can you think of a food you would like to break apart and "fix"? Now that you're an expert on sautéing veggies, we hope you'll enjoy testing out your new skill here.

PLAY WITH IT! Lots of different veggies taste great with chicken. You could add almost anything from the frozen section: broccoli, asparagus, peppers and different kinds of beans. How about small diced potatoes to make it more like a stew?

YIELD: 4 TO 6 SERVINGS

1 medium onion

2 cups (473 ml) milk

1 rotisserie chicken

3 tbsp (45 ml) olive oil

1 tsp jarred minced garlic

Sprinkle of salt & pepper

½ tsp dried thyme

¼ cup (25 g) all-purpose flour

1 (10-oz [284-g]) bag frozen mixed vegetables or mix 2 cups (459 g) of your own veggie variety including carrots, peas, green beans and corn

Biscuits or crackers, for serving (optional)

1. HEY KIDS, PLEASE GET US STARTED! ➤➤➤

Have your helper cut the onion into 4 large chunks so you can chop it into small-size pieces in a manual food processor.

Measure out the milk into a measuring cup, and set it aside.

Peel the skin off of the rotisserie chicken and throw it away. Using your fingers or a fork, shred the rotisserie chicken meat (both white breast meat and dark thigh meat) into small bite-size pieces.

2. PARENTS, ←—— IT'S YOUR TURN!

In a large saucepan, heat the olive oil over medium heat.

3. TEAMWORK GETS IT DONE!

Add the onion, garlic, salt, pepper and thyme to the pan, and stir to combine with a long-handled spoon. Heat until the onions are softened and translucent (clear), about 3 to 5 minutes.

With a whisk ready in the adult helper's hand, add the flour to the pan while the adult helper quickly stirs to combine with the onion mixture. Whisk continuously for 1 minute to toast the flour. The combination will quickly become dry and crumbly, but keep whisking to cook the flour through.

While the adult helper continues to whisk, gently pour the milk into the pot. Use the whisk to scrape up any dried bits of flour that may be clinging to the bottom of the pan. Turn the heat up to medium-high and continue to whisk the milk until thickened, about 5 minutes.

Turn the heat to low. Add the shredded chicken meat to the pot and stir to combine.

Add the bag of frozen vegetables to the pot. The heat from the sauce will finish thawing the veggies. Gently stir to combine and cover the pot with a lid. Periodically stir and heat until the veggies are cooked through, 3 to 5 minutes.

Serve the chicken potpie mixture in large bowls with some fresh biscuits, bread or crackers on the side if you like.

OLD WORLD TOMATO BEEF STEW

Our kids love to make this when grandma and grandpa come to visit because it gets grandma talking about the German foods she enjoyed as a young girl. Grandpa goes crazy for the caraway seeds, so we always set extras out on the table for him. Be sure to ask the adults at your table to share their own memories of their favorite childhood foods. Maybe this will be one of your new favorites! This stew makes the whole house smell comforting and cozy. Serve it with some fresh bread and a simple green salad.

PLAY WITH IT! Wavy egg noodles are our favorites, but this would be great with elbow macaroni or over spaghetti, too! Maybe try it stuffed into a baked potato with a little cheddar cheese. Frozen peas would be great if you mix them in after the tomatoes.

YIELD: 6 TO 8 SERVINGS

16 oz (454 g) wavy egg noodles

1 tsp cumin

1 tbsp (7 g) smoked paprika

1 tsp dried marjoram

¼ tsp nutmeg

Sprinkle of salt & pepper

1 small onion

1 green bell pepper

4 tbsp (57 g) butter

1 tbsp (8 g) caraway seeds

2 lb (907 g) ground beef

2 tsp (7 g) jarred garlic

1 (14-oz [397-g]) can of crushed tomatoes

¼ cup (60 ml) sour cream, plus more for serving

1. HEY KIDS, PLEASE GET US STARTED!

Have your helper put a large pot of water on to boil, and cook the noodles according to the directions on the package. While the noodles are cooking, measure out the cumin, paprika, marjoram, nutmeg, salt and pepper, and place them in a small bowl near the stove.

Have your adult helper cut the onion into 4 large chunks. Have your helper cut open the green pepper and remove the seeds. You can then chop the onion and pepper up into small pieces using a manual food processor.

After your helper has drained the pasta, measure and add the butter to the empty pot over medium heat. Once the butter is melted, stir in the cooked pasta until coated. Ask your helper to pour the buttered noodles into a large serving bowl, and then you can sprinkle them with the caraway seeds. Set the dish aside.

With the empty pot over medium heat, add the ground beef and crumble it up with a spoon as it browns. Once it is no longer pink, add the chopped onions and peppers, then measure and add the garlic. Stir together and cook until the onions are translucent (clear), about 5 minutes.

Add the seasonings to the beef mixture. Stir to combine, and cook for 1 minute.

Pour the crushed tomatoes into the pot and stir to combine with the beef. Cover the pot with a lid, and have your helper turn the heat down to medium-low. Let simmer for 10 to 20 minutes until heated through.

2. PARENTS, IT'S YOUR TURN!

Your kid chef will be able to do most of this recipe, but you will want to help them by managing the boiling water, transferring the hot pasta, cutting open the onion and pepper and draining the fat off the browned ground beef if there is too much liquid in the pot.

3. TEAMWORK GETS IT DONE!

Once the beef is done, add the sour cream to the mix. Stir it in until completely combined. Serve the stew spooned over the buttered noodles. You can garnish it with an additional dollop of sour cream, if you like.

COZY COUNTRY POTATO PIE

This is one of the coziest comfort foods we can think to make on a chilly weekend afternoon. While it simmers away inside the oven, you could have a family game night. The dish comes together quickly by using store-bought, prepared mashed potatoes. You can find them in the refrigerated section at the grocery store. Plain or sour cream and chive flavored potatoes would both be equally delicious here.

PLAY WITH IT! This is a pretty traditional version of what is also known as a shepherd's pie. If you wanted to play with it, you could add other veggies to the mix such as corn, green beans or peppers. Instead of the mashed potato topping, you could stir chunks of red potatoes into the beef mixture before baking. Or how about swapping mashed sweet potatoes for the regular ones?

YIELD: 6 TO 8 SERVINGS

2 small onions

2 carrots

2 slices sandwich bread

¼ cup (59 ml) milk

2 lb (907 g) ground beef

1½ cups (355 ml) chicken broth

¼ cup (59 ml) heavy cream

1 tbsp (15 ml) soy sauce

¼ cup (59 ml) vegetable oil

3 tsp (9 g) jarred minced garlic

1 tsp dried thyme

3 tbsp (46 g) tomato paste

⅓ cup (33 g) all-purpose flour

1 cup (151 g) frozen peas

3 cups (632 g) prepared mashed potatoes

1. HEY KIDS, PLEASE GET US STARTED! ➤——→

Have your adult helper cut the onions into quarters so you can chop them up into small pieces using a manual food processor. Then have your helper wash and peel the carrots, and cut them into small diced pieces.

Tear the sandwich bread into small pieces and add them to a large mixing bowl. Measure and add the milk and ground beef, and mash it all together with a fork.

Measure the chicken broth, pour it into a small bowl or cup, and set it near the stove. Then measure the heavy cream and add the soy sauce. Set them near the stove.

2. PARENTS, ←——— IT'S YOUR TURN!

When your kid chef asks, cut the carrots into a small dice.

Set a Dutch oven over medium-high heat. Preheat the oven to 325°F (170°C, or gas mark 3).

3. TEAMWORK GETS IT DONE!

Measure and add the vegetable oil to the Dutch oven, and let it preheat for a few minutes. Add the ground beef mixture and cook it until browned, about 8 to 10 minutes. Be sure to break it up with a spoon so it cooks evenly. When the beef is no longer pink, have the adult transfer it to a large bowl or plate. Set it aside.

Reduce the heat to medium-low, and add the onions and carrots to the pot. Measure and add the garlic and thyme. Stir them together and cook until the onions are softened, about 3 to 5 minutes. Measure and add the tomato paste to the pot, and stir to combine with the veggies. Measure and add the flour to the pot, and briskly stir for 1 minute. The mixture will quickly get sticky.

Whisk in the chicken broth and scrape up the browned bits from the bottom of the pan.

Return the ground beef mix to the pot and stir. Pour in the cream and soy sauce, and stir. Place the lid on the pot and bake in the oven for 1 hour.

Measure and stir in the peas. While the peas are cooking through, heat the prepared potatoes for 2 to 3 minutes in the microwave according to the directions on the package.

Stir the warmed potatoes, and then spoon them over the top of the beef. Use the back of a spoon or a spatula to smooth them into a solid layer over the top. Cover the pot and return it to the oven for 20 minutes.

Scoop large spoonfuls of the dish into bowls for serving.

TROPICAL SAUSAGES, PINEAPPLES, PEPPERS AND ONIONS

When winter feels like it is never going to end, we love to make this one-pan tropical recipe and pretend we're living on an island. It goes really well with Cilantro Lime Rice (page 160). Or, you can even serve this as a fun snack or appetizer when you have guests.

PLAY WITH IT! Roasted vegetables are so yummy! What else could you add to this mixture? Maybe next time try adding or swapping broccoli, zucchini, tomatoes, green beans or asparagus.

YIELD: 4 SERVINGS

1 (4 or 6-link) package of pineapple-flavored chicken sausages

1 red bell pepper

1 small red onion

1 fresh pineapple or 1 (20-oz [567-g]) can of pineapple chunks

2 tbsp (30 ml) olive oil

Salt & pepper

1. HEY KIDS, PLEASE GET US STARTED!

Set out a large cookie sheet near your cutting board. Open up the package of chicken sausages. Cut the sausage links into thick slices and place them on one end of the cookie sheet. If your butter knife doesn't work, you can ask your adult helper to finish this task.

Ask your adult helper to cut the red bell pepper open and remove the seeds. Cut the pepper into large chunks with a butter knife and place them on the cookie sheet.

Cut the onion into thick wedges and place them on the cookie sheet. If your butter knife doesn't work, you can ask your adult helper to finish this task.

Have your helper trim and core the fresh pineapple for you. Then you can cut it into large chunks with the butter knife, and place them on the cookie sheet. If you use canned pineapple, open the can and use the lid to drain the juices from the fruit before using them.

Drizzle the olive oil over all the vegetables and fruit, and gently toss them together with your hands until everything is nice and coated. Wash and dry your hands.

Sprinkle salt and pepper over the vegetable mixture.

2. PARENTS, IT'S YOUR TURN!

Preheat the oven to 425°F (220°C, or gas mark 7).

Assist your kid chef with cutting the vegetables when asked. Trim and core the fresh pineapple, if using.

3. TEAMWORK GETS IT DONE!

Bake the sausages and veggies for 30 to 40 minutes, tossing the veggies and flipping the sausage slices after 15 to 20 minutes to make sure nothing burns on the bottom.

Serve the sausages and veggies on a large platter. They taste great warm or even at room temperature!

MINI MEATBALL SKILLET

These yummy meatballs are the ultimate "play with your food" food! Mix the filling together and roll the balls out with your hands. It's better than playing with Play-Doh because you can dip your breadsticks in the delicious sauce and gobble them up when you're done. Add a simple salad as a side dish and this is a perfectly well-rounded meal.

PLAY WITH IT! You could add several different seasonings to the meatball mix: basil, thyme, oregano or red pepper flakes would all be delicious with the marinara. Or you can turn this into a completely different kind of dish and season them with your favorite Mexican blend of spices. Add some onions and peppers to the tomato sauce, and then sprinkle with some fresh cilantro.

YIELD: 4 TO 6 SERVINGS

½ cup (60 g) panko breadcrumbs

2 tbsp (30 ml) milk

1 egg

1 lb (454 g) ground beef (OR ½ lb [227 g] ground beef mixed with ½ lb [227 g] ground pork)

1 tsp jarred minced garlic

1 tbsp (3 g) parsley

½ tsp nutmeg

3 tbsp (34 g) Parmesan cheese

Salt & pepper

1 tbsp (15 ml) olive oil

1 (24-oz [656 ml]) jar marinara sauce

1 cup (121 g) mozzarella cheese

Breadsticks, for serving

1. HEY KIDS, PLEASE GET US STARTED!

Measure and add the breadcrumbs and milk to a large mixing bowl, and stir them together. Give the crumbs a minute to soak up the milk, and mush it all together with a fork.

Crack the egg into a small cup and whisk it with a fork to break the yolk. Stir until light yellow.

Measure and add the ground beef, garlic, parsley, nutmeg, Parmesan cheese, a sprinkle of salt and pepper and the egg to the mixing bowl. Use your hands to gently combine all the ingredients. Don't overmix the beef or it will get tough. Just lightly turn the meat until all the seasonings are well mixed throughout the beef.

Pinch off portions of meat just smaller than a golf ball, and roll them in your hands. Line the formed meatballs on a plate.

2. PARENTS, IT'S YOUR TURN!

Set a skillet over medium heat. Add the olive oil to the pan.

3. TEAMWORK GETS IT DONE!

Add the meatballs to the skillet and brown them on all sides, about 5 to 7 minutes. Reduce heat to medium-low, and pour in the jar of marinara sauce. Cover the skillet with a lid. Simmer the meatballs in the sauce for 15 to 20 minutes, or until the meatballs are cooked through. Turn the heat off.

Sprinkle the meatballs with the mozzarella cheese, and let the cheese melt as the meatballs rest for 10 minutes.

Serve alongside fresh breadsticks for dunking.

CLASSIC FRENCH BEEF STEW

A very special lady named Julia Child made a similar stew very famous. She was fearless in the kitchen, and she didn't let any mistakes stop her. I hope you'll learn to be like Julia. We took notes from her recipe and made it a lot easier for modern families and tastier for kids. This is a perfect snow day meal when you want to be warm and cozy.

PLAY WITH IT! This recipe is a little harder to play with, but not impossible! You can add any root vegetable you like to the veggie mix. Sweet potatoes, parsnips, turnips or rutabagas would all work with the carrots and potatoes. You could also add butternut squash, green beans or mushrooms later in the cooking.

YIELD: 6 TO 8 SERVINGS

3 carrots

½ lb (227 g) baby potatoes

2 tbsp (30 ml) red wine vinegar

1½ cups (355 ml) chicken broth

2 tbsp (30 ml) soy sauce

4 slices bacon

1½ lb (680 g) precut stew beef

1 tsp jarred minced garlic

1 tbsp (2 g) thyme

2 tsp (10 g) tomato paste

2 tbsp (12 g) all-purpose flour

Fresh bread or prepared mashed potatoes, for serving (optional)

1. HEY KIDS, PLEASE GET US STARTED! ➤➤→

Wash and peel the carrots, and scrub the potatoes. Ask your adult helper to cut them for you.

Measure the red wine vinegar, chicken broth and soy sauce in a large measuring cup. Give it a stir to combine.

2. PARENTS, ←◄ IT'S YOUR TURN!

When your kid chef asks, cut the carrots into large chunks and the potatoes into halves or quarters, depending on their size.

Cut the bacon into chunks.

Put a Dutch oven on the stove top over medium-high heat, and preheat the oven to 300°F (150°C, or gas mark 2).

3. TEAMWORK GETS IT DONE!

Add the bacon to the pot, and give it a quick stir. Let it brown and crisp up. When the white part (the fat) has melted into the pot, about 5 to 7 minutes, remove the bacon with a slotted spoon and place it on a plate for later.

The adult helper should add the stew beef to the pot in small batches and brown it on all sides. If you overcrowd the pan, it will boil instead of brown. If the adult helper approves, you can help stir each batch of beef. Once it is browned on the outside, about 5 minutes per batch, use your slotted spoon to remove the beef to the same plate as the bacon. Once all the beef has been browned, add the carrots and potatoes to the pot. Measure and add in the garlic and thyme.

Cook the veggies for 2 to 3 minutes. Then measure and stir in the tomato paste. Measure and sprinkle the flour over the veggies, and stir to combine. Cook for 1 to 2 minutes and then pour in the chicken broth mixture. Stir and scrape the bottom of the pan to get all the browned bits up and smooth out the lumps from the flour.

Add the bacon and beef back to the pot, and stir to combine with the broth. Place the lid on the pot, and bake it in the oven for 2 hours. The pot will be hot and heavy—don't forget to wear oven mitts and let the adult helper handle the transfer in and out of the oven.

The stew is delicious on its own, or serve it over prepared mashed potatoes or with fresh bread.

SLOW COOKER JAMBALAYA

When you want your comfort food a little spicier, this southern jambalaya is the answer. Usually it has a trio of meats: chicken, sausage and shrimp. But if you only want one or two of those? I won't tell. This yummy stew can be enjoyed all by itself, over rice or with bread for dunking.

PLAY WITH IT! The sausage used here comes in all ranges of spicy. Pick your favorite! You can adjust the seasonings to be more or less spicy, or swap in some bottled hot sauce instead of the Cajun blend.

YIELD: 6 TO 8 SERVINGS

1 onion

1 green bell pepper

2 celery ribs

14 oz (397 g) smoked or andouille sausage

2 (14.5-oz [411-g]) cans of diced tomatoes

3 tsp (9 g) jarred minced garlic

2 cups (473 ml) chicken stock

2 tsp (10 ml) Worcestershire sauce

2 bay leaves

2 tbsp (30 g) Cajun seasoning

2 tsp (8 g) sugar

2 tsp (1 g) oregano

1 tsp dried basil

½ tsp dried thyme

1 tbsp (3 g) parsley

1 lb (454 g) chicken tenderloins or boneless, skinless thighs

1 lb (454 g) raw shrimp, peeled, deveined, tails removed

Prepared plain white rice, for serving (optional)

1. HEY KIDS, PLEASE GET US STARTED!

Have your parent helper cut the onion, green bell pepper and celery into large chunks so you can chop them with your manual food processor. Work one veggie at a time so you don't overcrowd your machine.

Cut the sausage into bite-size chunks using your butter knife. Ask for help if you need it.

Open the can of tomatoes and pour them into the slow cooker. Measure and add the garlic, chicken stock, Worcestershire sauce, bay leaves and all the seasonings. Stir it all together.

2. PARENTS, IT'S YOUR TURN!

Prepare the veggies for your kid chef when asked.

Cut the chicken into bite-size chunks.

3. TEAMWORK GETS IT DONE!

Add the prepared veggies and the sausage and chicken to the slow cooker, and stir to combine them with the sauce.

Cook on low for 7 to 8 hours or on high for 4 hours.

In the last 10 minutes, add the shrimp to the slow cooker and stir them in. Look for and remove the bay leaves. Let the shrimp simmer in the pot for 10 minutes, until pink and cooked through.

Serve the jambalaya as a hearty stew or over plain white rice.

FESTA ♥ ITALIANA

Pizza or pasta tonight? How awesome it would be to live in a country that got to ask that question every single day! Though, you would soon discover that Italian food is more than just pepperoni pizza or buttered noodles. The varieties for both are endless.

In this chapter, basic building-block recipes for pasta sauce that you can customize are mixed with a few American-style spin-offs. You'll see all the creative ways you can play with everyone's favorite Italian dishes.

Maybe start with the classic Super Simple Spaghetti & Tomato Sauce (page 132) before diving in with the more modern Buffalo Chicken Pasta (page 140). Or mix things up and serve your family the mouthwatering BBQ Chicken Pizza (page 146). You're going to love learning how to roll out homemade pizza dough for the crust!

Fettuccini

Farfalle Butterflies

Rotini / Fusilli

Shells

Spaghetti

You've Got Skills

CHOOSING AND COOKING NOODLES

Did you know that there are over 300 different kinds of pasta shapes in the world? What we see on the shelf at the store is just a tiny portion of what is created for noodle lovers everywhere.

How do you know which pasta shape to pair with your recipe? The truth is that you can use whatever you like, but traditionally there are a few rules if you want to follow them.

SHORT PASTAS: These shapes do really well with heartier sauces that involve bits of meat or chunks of veggies. Which one do you think would trap a green pea the best?

1. Farfalle butterflies
2. Penne
3. Rigatoni
4. Campanelle
5. Cellentani
6. Rotini / Fusilli

LONG PASTAS: For thinner and smoother sauces, long pasta shapes are the way to go. The biggest difference between them is their width. The creamier and heavier the sauce, the wider the noodle you want to go with it.

1. Angel hair
2. Spaghetti
3. Fettuccini
4. Linguine

FUN PASTA SHAPES: These fun shapes are perfect for soups or for homemade macaroni and cheese.

1. Shells
2. Wagon wheels / Rotelle
3. Ditalini
4. Stellini
5. Orzo

Each pasta shape requires its own cooking time, but the method is the same.

1. Fill a large pot two-thirds full with water. Place it over a stove-top burner turned to high heat.

2. Add several pinches of salt to the water, this will help to season the pasta as it cooks.

3. Wait for the water to come to a boil. When it is nice and bubbly, carefully pour your pasta into the hot water. It's a great idea to wear baking gloves to protect your bare hands from any hot water splashes.

4. Stir the pasta immediately to prevent it from sticking to the bottom of the pot.

5. Set a timer for the lower end of the cooking time that is listed on your pasta package. This will give you pasta al dente, which means "to the tooth." The pasta will cook a little more when you add it to the sauce, so you want to be sure it isn't overdone right from the pot.

6. Have your adult helper drain the pasta before using it in the rest of your recipe.

BETTER THAN BUTTERED NOODLES

Buttered noodles are a Children's Menu staple at most restaurants. I know it is probably already one of your very favorite dinners, especially when it's made with your favorite shape of pasta. It's also the perfect simple dinner to really play around with inventing your own recipe. Think of all the different things you could add to spice it up! How many combinations can you make?

YIELD: 4 TO 6 SERVINGS

COOKING OIL
6 tbsp (86 g) butter, olive oil or a combination

TWO OR THREE VEGGIES (USE 1 CUP OF EACH; WEIGHT WILL VARY)
Frozen peas

Frozen corn

Zucchini slices

Broccoli, chopped

Bell peppers, chunks

SEASONINGS (USE ONE OR MORE)
1 tsp garlic salt

Sprinkle of red pepper flakes

1 tsp basil

1 tsp thyme

1 tsp chives

MEAT (USE 1–2 CUPS; WEIGHT WILL VARY)
Rotisserie chicken, shredded

Chopped deli ham

Sautéed sausage slices

PASTA
1 (16-oz [454-g]) box pasta, boiled and drained

FINISHING FLAVOR (OPTIONAL)
Parmesan cheese

Mozzarella cheese

Lemon juice

1. HEY KIDS, PLEASE GET US STARTED!

Add the butter and/or olive oil to the same pot you used to make your pasta. Turn the heat to medium, and melt the butter.

Add the prepared veggies you selected to the butter, and sprinkle them with the seasonings you picked out. Sauté them until the veggies are just softened.

Add the shredded or chopped meat to the veggies and stir them together. Heat for 1 to 2 minutes until everything is warmed through.

2. PARENTS, IT'S YOUR TURN!

Add the pasta back to the pot.

3. TEAMWORK GETS IT DONE!

Toss the pasta together with the veggies and the meat until the pasta is coated in butter. Let the pasta sauté for 5 minutes so it soaks up the butter. Give it a gentle stir every couple of minutes to keep it from sticking to the bottom of the pot.

Serve the buttered pasta dish sprinkled with cheese or lemon juice (if using) over the top.

SUPER SIMPLE SPAGHETTI & TOMATO SAUCE

Making your own spaghetti sauce couldn't be easier, but you don't have to use it on spaghetti! This is a great recipe for testing out a new shape you'd like to try. It's quite possible you have everything you need for the sauce already sitting in your pantry.

PLAY WITH IT! Notice how this recipe has no seasonings listed? You can add almost any Italian seasonings you like: garlic, basil, thyme, oregano or even rosemary. The blend you choose makes this sauce your own.

YIELD: 6 SERVINGS

1 (16-oz [454-g]) box of your favorite pasta shape

1 (28-oz [794-g]) can of crushed tomatoes

1 small onion

5 tbsp (72 g) butter

Sprinkle of salt

Parmesan cheese, for serving

1. HEY KIDS, PLEASE GET US STARTED!

Before you make the sauce, get your pasta ready. Ask your adult helper to put a large pot of salted water over high heat, and bring it to a boil. Add the box of pasta to the water, and cook it according to the lowest time listed on the package. Have your adult helper drain the pasta and set it aside for later. Return the pot to the stove top for making the sauce.

While your helper drains the cooked pasta, open the can of crushed tomatoes. Peel the outer wrapping off an onion. Ask your helper to cut it in half.

Measure the butter, and set it by the stove.

2. PARENTS, IT'S YOUR TURN!

Boil the pasta and drain it for your kid chef. Let it rest in the colander while your kid chef prepares the sauce.

Return the pot to the stove over medium-high heat. Cut the onion in half when your kid chef asks.

3. TEAMWORK GETS IT DONE!

Melt the butter in the same pot you used to boil the pasta. Pour in the crushed tomatoes, add a sprinkle of salt and stir. Place the onion in the pot cut-side down. Simmer the sauce gently for 45 minutes. Scoop out and discard the onion.

Add the prepared pasta to the pot and gently toss it with the hot sauce to warm it through. Serve with a sprinkle of Parmesan cheese.

HEARTY ITALIAN RAGÙ MEAT SAUCE

If you are looking for a meatier sauce for your favorite pasta, or as a topping for some gnocchi, this sweet Italian ragù is perfect. The veggies that give it so much flavor are diced up teeny tiny, and after they've simmered for an hour, you hardly know they are there.

PLAY WITH IT! The base of this recipe is beef and pork, but you can use ground turkey if you want to make a lighter dish. You could add bacon, chopped sun-dried tomatoes, bell peppers or a splash of balsamic vinegar.

YIELD: 6 TO 8 SERVINGS

1 (1-lb [454-g]) box of your favorite pasta shape

1 onion

2 celery ribs

1 carrot

½ cup (118 ml) whole milk

2 tbsp (30 ml) red wine vinegar

½ cup (118 ml) beef stock

4 tsp (13 g) jarred minced garlic

½ tsp nutmeg

½ tsp dried thyme

2 tbsp (30 ml) olive oil

½ lb (227 g) ground beef

½ lb (227 g) ground pork

1 (6-oz [170-g]) can of tomato paste

Parmesan cheese, for serving

1. HEY KIDS, PLEASE GET US STARTED!

Ask your helper to set a large pot of salted water over high heat to bring it to a boil. Add the box of pasta to the water, and cook it according to the lowest time listed on the package. Have your adult helper drain the pasta and set it aside for later. Return the pot to the stove top for making the sauce.

Ask your adult helper to cut the onion, celery and carrot into quarters or large chunks so you can chop them up using a manual food processor. Work one veggie at a time so you don't overcrowd your chopper.

Measure the whole milk, red wine vinegar and beef stock in a large measuring cup. Stir them to combine, and set the cup near the stove.

Measure the garlic, nutmeg and thyme and put them together in a small bowl. Set the bowl near the stove.

2. PARENTS, IT'S YOUR TURN!

Boil the pasta and drain it for your kid chef. Set it aside for serving.

Prepare the veggies for your kid chef to chop in their manual food processor.

Set a large sauce pot over medium-high heat.

3. TEAMWORK GETS IT DONE!

Add the olive oil to the pot. After 1 minute, add the diced onions, celery and carrots to the pot and stir. Sprinkle them with salt & pepper and add the garlic and seasonings. Stir to combine.

Add the ground beef and ground pork to the pot. Stir and break the meat up into chunks so it cooks evenly. In about 10 minutes once it has browned and is no longer pink, add the tomato paste and stir. Add the milk mixture and stir. Heat the mixture until it starts to bubble and then cover the pot with a lid and reduce the heat to low. Simmer the sauce for 1 to 1½ hours.

Give the sauce a stir every 10 to 15 minutes to make sure nothing is sticking to the bottom of your pot.

Add the prepared pasta to the pot, and gently toss it with the hot sauce to warm it through. Serve with a sprinkle of Parmesan cheese.

PARMESAN GNOCCHI

We call these "pasta pillows" in our house. Gnocchi are little Italian dumplings made with potato, but they are light and fluffy, just like a pillow. They would be just perfect with the Bolognese sauce (page 134), but they also make a wonderful side dish or dinner entrée with simpler sauces.

PLAY WITH IT! You can change the seasonings here just as you would the Better Than Buttered Noodles (page 129). You could also add a squeeze of fresh lemon juice and some asparagus with the peas for a springtime version of the dish.

YIELD: 4 TO 6 SERVINGS

1 cup (151 g) frozen peas

½ tsp sage

½ tsp garlic salt

¼ tsp nutmeg

1 (1.1-lb [500-g]) package of gnocchi

4 tbsp (57 g) butter

½ cup (90 g) shredded Parmesan cheese

1. HEY KIDS, PLEASE GET US STARTED! ➤━━→

Measure the peas. Set them near the stove.

Measure the sage, garlic salt and nutmeg, and stir them into a little cup or bowl. Set them next to the peas.

2. PARENTS, ←━━■ IT'S YOUR TURN!

Set a large pot of salted water over high heat, and bring it to a boil.

3. TEAMWORK GETS IT DONE!

Add the gnocchi to the boiling water and stir. They only need about 2 to 3 minutes to cook; you'll know they're ready when they all float to the top of the water. Add the peas to the boiling water and stir. Let them soak for 1 minute. Have your adult helper drain the gnocchi and peas into a colander in the sink.

Return the empty pot to the stove and heat it over medium-low. Measure and add the butter to the pot to melt. Once the butter has melted, add the seasonings and stir.

Add the cooked gnocchi and peas to the pot and stir to coat them in butter. Let them sauté for a few minutes so they get a chance to absorb the butter.

Sprinkle the Parmesan cheese over the top, and serve.

SAUSAGE TORTELLINI WITH PEAS

Buttered noodles are a favorite first food for many kids. A fun next step can be playing with the seasonings and trying different shapes. These delicious sausage tortellini are kicked up just a notch with the addition of some warm nutmeg and spicy red pepper flakes.

PLAY WITH IT! Tortellini come in many different flavors: chicken, cheese, sausage and more! Experiment with which flavor you love the most. Frozen peas are easy to cook right in the same boiling water as the pasta, but you could use any frozen veggie you like. Asparagus, peppers, corn or broccoli would also be yummy.

YIELD: 4 TO 6 SERVINGS

1 (20-oz [567-g]) package of sausage-filled tortellini

1 (10.8-oz [306-g]) bag frozen peas

1 tsp garlic salt

1 tsp dried thyme

¼ tsp nutmeg

Generous sprinkle of red pepper flakes

6 tbsp (86 g) butter

Grated Parmesan cheese, for serving

1. HEY KIDS, PLEASE GET US STARTED!

Have your helper put a large pasta pot filled with salted water over high heat so it comes to a boil. Add the tortellini to the water, and cook for 4 minutes. Add the frozen peas to the boiling water and cook for an additional 1 to 2 minutes.

Have your helper drain the pasta and peas, and return the pot over medium heat.

While you're waiting for the water to boil, measure the garlic salt, thyme, nutmeg and red pepper flakes, and put them in a small bowl near the stove.

Measure and add the butter to the pot and let it melt. Then add the seasonings, and stir to combine it all with the butter. Add the drained pasta and peas back to the pot, and stir gently to coat the pasta with the butter.

Sauté the tortellini for a few minutes over medium-low heat.

2. PARENTS, IT'S YOUR TURN!

Assist your kid chef with boiling the water and draining the pasta. You may also want to transfer the pasta back to the hot pot once the butter has melted.

3. TEAMWORK GETS IT DONE!

Serve the pasta with Parmesan cheese sprinkled on top.

BUFFALO CHICKEN PASTA

Does your family all agree on how spicy to make your food? We sure don't. In our family, Dad devours anything buffalo flavored while the youngest of our kids would run for the hills if she spied red sauce on her plate! We invented this dinner to please everyone at the table. Serve up the mild and creamy chicken noodle base, and let everyone in your family choose whether it should be plain or Spice Level 10. And for the nervous-but-curious ones? Be sure to test the buffalo sauce with some raw veggies before pouring it all over your finished dish.

PLAY WITH IT! There's nothing spicy about this creamy sauce. You could add frozen peas, diced ham and a little lemon zest to make a fancy Alfredo dish instead.

YIELD: 4 TO 6 SERVINGS

1 lb (454 g) corkscrew shaped pasta

2 cups (473 ml) milk

½ cup (115 g) butter (1 stick)

1 (8-oz [227-g]) package of cream cheese

2 tsp (10 g) garlic salt

½ cup (90 g) ground Parmesan cheese

Sprinkle of black pepper

FOR SERVING

1 lb (454 g) cooked chicken tenderloins, chopped

2–3 green onions

Blue cheese crumbles

1 (12-oz [328-ml]) bottle prepared buffalo sauce

SUGGESTED SIDE DISHES

Raw celery sticks

Raw baby carrots

1. HEY KIDS, PLEASE GET US STARTED! ➤——→

Ask your adult helper to put a large pot of salted water over high heat, and bring it to a boil. Add the pasta to the pot and stir, cooking it for the shortest amount of time listed on the package. Ask the adult to drain the pasta into a colander and reserve for later. Return the pot to the stove top.

Meanwhile, measure the milk into a measuring cup, and set it near the stove.

Shred the chicken into bite-size pieces using your fingers. Place the meat on a plate or in a small bowl.

Remove the tips from both ends of the green onions with your butter knife. Then, cut the stalks into 4 shorter pieces, and chop the green onions into small pieces using a manual food processor. Put them in a small bowl on the table.

Lay the fresh veggies into a pretty pattern on a tray, and add them to the table. Add a spoon to the container of blue cheese crumbles, and put it and the bottle of buffalo sauce on the table so everyone can customize their own pasta.

Now, prepare the sauce. Measure and add the butter to the pot. Melt it over medium-high heat.

Add the cream cheese and garlic salt to the pot and stir while gently breaking up the brick of cheese with your cooking spoon.

When the cream cheese is halfway melted down, add the milk. Gently stir or whisk the mixture to keep the milk and cheese from sticking to the bottom of the pan.

Bring the sauce to a gentle bubble and whisk until it begins to thicken, about 8 to 10 minutes. Reduce the heat to low; measure and add the Parmesan cheese and black pepper. Stir to combine.

2. PARENTS, ←——◄ IT'S YOUR TURN!

Set a large pasta pot filled with water and a sprinkle of salt over high heat to bring to a boil. Cook the pasta in the boiling water according to the box directions. Strain the finished pasta and return the pot to the stove.

3. TEAMWORK GETS IT DONE!

Have the adult helper transfer half of the pasta sauce into a bowl or measuring cup, then transfer the pasta back to the sauce pot. Stir the pasta until coated with sauce. Add additional sauce until the pasta reaches your family's preferred consistency. (Any remaining sauce can be stored separately from the leftover pasta and used to rehydrate the dish when you reheat it, or to coat a new box of pasta for a second dinner.)

Add the chopped chicken to the pasta. Stir to coat, and heat it through.

Serve the pasta and the chicken mixture in large bowls, and let each family member add the green onions, blue cheese crumbles and buffalo sauce buffet-style to make their perfect combination.

You've Got Skills

HOW TO MAKE PIZZA DOUGH FROM SCRATCH AND ROLL IT OUT

You could buy a premade pizza crust at the store, but making homemade pizza from scratch is so fun. Everyone should try it at least once.

YIELD: 2 PIZZA CRUSTS

1¼ cups (296 ml) water at room temperature

½ cup (118 ml) warm water

2¼ tsp (7 g) instant yeast

4 cups (398 g) bread flour, plus more for dusting

1½ tsp (8 g) salt

2 tbsp (30 ml) olive oil + 1 tbsp (15 ml) for oiling a bowl

Sprinkle of all-purpose flour for the working surface

Parchment paper

Sprinkle of cornmeal for the rolling surface

1. HEY KIDS, PLEASE GET US STARTED! ➤——→

Measure 1¼ cup (296 ml) of water and pour it into a small bowl. Set the bowl on your counter, and let it come to room temperature for 10 minutes.

Measure ½ cup (118 ml) of warm water into a liquid measuring cup. Sprinkle the yeast over the top of the water.

Ask your helper to set a stand mixer on your counter, and be sure it has the paddle attachment hooked up. Measure and add the bread flour and salt to the bowl of the mixer, and stir it together to blend.

Add the bowl of room temperature water to the cup with the yeast. Measure and add 2 tablespoons (30 ml) of olive oil to the cup.

Pour 1 tablespoon (15 ml) of olive oil into a large mixing bowl. Use your fingers to spread the oil all over the surface of the inside of the bowl. Set the bowl aside. Wash your hands.

Turn the mixer on to low speed. Pour the water-oil-yeast mixture in with the flour. Mix everything together until a dough is formed. Switch the paddle attachment to the dough hook. Knead on low speed for 5 minutes until the dough is smooth and stretchy.

Move the dough into the oiled mixing bowl, and turn it over once to coat it in oil. Cover the bowl with plastic wrap, and let the dough rise until it has doubled in size. This will take about 1½ to 2 hours.

When the dough has risen, remove the plastic wrap, and press down on the dough to deflate it. Sprinkle some flour over your working surface, and place the dough on top.

Divide the dough into 2 equal pieces. Form each piece into a smooth, round ball. (You can freeze the pizza dough wrapped in plastic wrap at this point, if you like.) Cover the dough with a damp paper towel and let it relax for 10 to 30 minutes.

2. PARENTS, ←——◄ IT'S YOUR TURN!

Place a pizza stone on the middle rack, and preheat the oven to 500°F (260°C) for 30 minutes.

3. TEAMWORK GETS IT DONE!

If you don't have a wooden pizza peel that came with your pizza stone, use the back side of a cookie sheet or a flat wooden cutting board to roll out your pizza dough.

Place a large piece of parchment paper on your rolling surface, and then sprinkle it with some cornmeal. Rub some flour into your hands and then place the dough on top of the rolling surface. Gently shape the dough into a round pizza circle. The dough should be even across the surface, but it's okay to leave it a little thicker around the edge for a crust.

Brush the outer edge of the crust with some olive oil. Add your sauce and toppings. Have your adult helper slide the parchment paper with the pizza on top off the rolling surface and onto the hot stone in the oven. Bake until the crust is golden brown and the cheese is bubbly, 8 to 12 minutes.

PESTO PIZZA WITH FRESH TOMATOES

Pesto is made mostly from fresh basil, olive oil and Parmesan cheese. It smells like summer in a jar. You can grow a forest of basil really easily on your patio or even in a windowsill to make your own, or buy prepared pesto from the grocery store. It's fantastic on top of pasta, but we love to use it to make "green pizza."

PLAY WITH IT! Stick with the green theme and play with how many green veggies you could add to your pizza. Green peppers, chopped broccoli, asparagus or spinach would all be yummy with the pesto. You could add some cooked chicken or sausage, too. If you want pizza with a little kick, add some roasted red pepper flakes to your serving.

YIELD: 8 SERVINGS

1 ball of pizza dough (page 142) or 1 prepared pizza crust

Parchment paper

½–1 cup (123–245 g) prepared pesto

3 cups (539 g) mozzarella cheese

1 cup (180 g) shredded Parmesan cheese

2 Roma tomatoes

1. HEY KIDS, PLEASE GET US STARTED!

Follow the instructions on page 143 to roll out your pizza dough on a piece of parchment.

Measure and spread the pesto over the surface of the pizza crust, leaving a small bit of room around the edge for the crust.

Measure and sprinkle the mozzarella cheese and Parmesan cheese over the pesto. Spread them evenly with your fingers.

Ask your adult helper to slice the tomatoes.

2. PARENTS, IT'S YOUR TURN!

Preheat the oven to 500°F (260°C) with a pizza stone on the middle rack. If using a prepared pizza crust, follow the instructions on the package.

When your kid chef asks, slice the tomatoes into thin slices.

3. TEAMWORK GETS IT DONE!

Lay the tomato slices over the top of the pizza.

The adult helper should transfer the pizza on top of the parchment paper to the oven. Bake for 8 to 12 minutes. The pizza is ready when the cheese is melted, the tomatoes are roasted and the crust is golden brown.

Carefully slide the pizza off the stone and onto a cutting board or baking sheet. Slice and serve.

BBQ CHICKEN PIZZA

When you want a tomato-based sauce for your pizza but are in the mood for something a little bit different, barbecue sauce is an amazing substitution. This sweet and spicy pizza is a yummier version of a barbecue sandwich.

PLAY WITH IT! You can use any prepared sauce you love for this recipe. Have someone who wants peppers and someone who doesn't? Add them to just half of the top of the pizza. Same for the onions.

YIELD: 8 SERVINGS

1 ball of pizza dough (page 142) or
1 prepared pizza crust

Parchment paper

½–1 cup (118–237 ml) prepared
barbecue sauce

1 cup (227 g) chunks of cooked
chicken tenderloins

3 cups (539 g) shredded mozzarella
cheese

1 cup (121 g) shredded cheddar
cheese

1 green pepper

1 red onion or 3-4 green onions

1 bunch fresh cilantro

1. HEY KIDS, PLEASE GET US STARTED!

Follow the instructions on page 142 to roll out your pizza dough on a piece of parchment.

Measure and spread the barbecue sauce over the surface of the pizza crust, leaving a small bit of room around the edge for the crust.

Measure and sprinkle the mozzarella cheese and cheddar cheese over the barbecue sauce.

Spread them evenly with your fingers.

Have your adult helper cut the pepper and onion into large chunks so you can chop them up with a manual food processor. Sprinkle them over the top of the pizza.

Finally, add the chopped chicken chunks evenly over the pizza.

2. PARENTS, IT'S YOUR TURN!

Preheat the oven to 500°F (260°C) with a pizza stone on the middle rack. If using a prepared pizza crust, follow the instructions on the package.

Chop the pepper and onion into chunks when asked, and let your kid chef chop them up into little pieces.

Chop the cilantro.

3. TEAMWORK GETS IT DONE!

The adult helper should transfer the pizza on the parchment paper to the oven. Bake for 8 to 12 minutes. The pizza is ready when the cheese is melted, the tomatoes are roasted and the crust is golden brown.

Carefully slide the pizza and parchment paper onto a cutting board or baking sheet.

Sprinkle the top with the fresh cilantro, slice and serve.

MAKE ♥ YOUR OWN RESTAURANT FOOD

You could go out to a restaurant to get your favorite food, or you could make it even more perfect by preparing it exactly your way right at home. Try our Chicken Finger Dunkers (page 150) or the Teeny-Weeny Cheeseburger Sliders (page 152) next time you're hankering for the drive-thru. Want something a little spicier? Don't miss the Pineapple Cashew Fried Rice (page 162) or our favorite Potsticker Stir-Fry (page 164).

Do you have a special restaurant that makes something you love a certain way? Try to replicate it in your own kitchen. Next time you eat out, make a note in your memory about what you'd like to try to improve on yourself.

CHICKEN FINGER DUNKERS

Chicken fingers at restaurants are usually deep fried and not very healthy. This baked version is easy to make at home, and it has a lot more flavor. Plus, you know it's real chicken tucked inside the crunchy coating! This recipe is perfect for dunking in your favorite condiments, but we love honey mustard the best.

PLAY WITH IT! You could make spicy chicken fingers by changing the seasoning in the flour or adding a little hot sauce to the eggs.

YIELD: 4 SERVINGS

CHICKEN FINGERS

½ cup (50 g) all-purpose flour

1 tbsp (15 g) seasoned salt

3 eggs

1 tbsp (16 g) mustard

1 cup (121 g) panko breadcrumbs

1 lb (454 g) boneless, skinless chicken tenderloins

Cooking spray

HONEY MUSTARD (FOR SERVING)

2 tbsp (30 ml) honey

2 tbsp (32 g) mustard

1. HEY KIDS, PLEASE GET US STARTED! ➤➤

Place 2 rimmed plates and 1 medium bowl on the counter. On the first plate, measure and add the flour and the seasoned salt. Use a fork to stir them together.

Crack the eggs into the bowl, being watchful for any bits of shell that might sneak in. Use a fork to break the yolks, and gently whisk the eggs together. Measure and add the mustard, and whisk again.

Measure and pour the breadcrumbs on the second plate.

Place the chicken on the left and a baking sheet to the right of the 3 dishes. Now your assembly line is ready.

2. PARENTS, ◄◄ IT'S YOUR TURN!

Preheat the oven to 450°F (230°C, or gas mark 8).

3. TEAMWORK GETS IT DONE!

Each chicken tenderloin needs to be dipped and coated in flour, then dipped and coated in egg, and finally dipped and coated in breadcrumbs and laid on the baking sheet.

Be sure to let the excess egg run off the chicken before placing it into the breadcrumbs. To keep things neat, use one hand to move the chicken in and out of the eggs and the other hand for patting the breadcrumbs into place.

If you don't want to touch the chicken with your hands, you can also use forks or tongs to move the chicken through the assembly line.

Spray the tops of the prepared chicken fingers with the cooking spray. Bake for 6 minutes and then flip the chicken over and spritz with a little more cooking oil. Bake for another 6 minutes until the chicken is cooked through and reaches 180°F (82°C).

While the chicken is cooking, prepare the honey mustard. Measure and mix the honey and mustard together in a small bowl, and place it on your table for serving.

TEENY-WEENY CHEESEBURGER SLIDERS

Grilling up hamburgers is fun in the summer, but what about the rest of the year? These little burgers are perfect for making indoors any time. Hawaiian rolls are slightly sweetened and delicious for sliders. If you can't find them, you can substitute any small roll you have available.

PLAY WITH IT! A burger is a blank palette for any topping you like. Mix your favorites: tomatoes, bacon, pineapple, barbecue sauce, ranch dressing, blue cheese, cheddar cheese or Swiss cheese.

YIELD: 4 SERVINGS

1 lb (454 g) ground beef

1 tbsp (15 g) Montreal steak seasoning

1 tsp Worcestershire sauce

1 tsp mustard

8 mini Hawaiian rolls or mini potato buns

4 slices of cheese

1. HEY KIDS, PLEASE GET US STARTED!

Line a broiling pan with tinfoil and set it aside.

Place the ground beef in a large mixing bowl. Measure and add the Montreal steak seasoning, Worcestershire sauce and mustard to the beef. Use a fork to gently mix everything together.

Divide the beef mixture equally into 8 portions. Take 1 portion at a time and roll it into a small ball. Then gently pat the ball into a disc to form a little hamburger patty. Place the patties on the broiling pan.

2. PARENTS, IT'S YOUR TURN!

Preheat the broiler with a rack positioned so that the broiling pan will be 3 inches (8 cm) away from the heating element.

Slice the rolls if they are not precut.

3. TEAMWORK GETS IT DONE!

Broil the hamburgers for 3 minutes on the first side and then flip them over. Continue to broil them for an additional 5 minutes, or until they reach a minimum of 160°F (71°C) in the middle when you test with a meat thermometer.

Add half of each slice of cheese to the top of each burger patty. Return them to the broiler for 20 seconds, or until just melted.

Place 1 patty on each mini bun and serve.

MIX AND MATCH SEASONED FRENCH FRIES

Do you like your french fries plain or seasoned? You can make them exactly how you like them when you bake them at home. You can even make half the batch seasoned one way, the other half seasoned another way to please everyone at the table. Crunchy, crispy and so much tastier than at a restaurant!

PLAY WITH IT! You can spice up these fries any way you like! Any of the seasoning blends from the popcorn recipe on page 192 would work great, or you can make up your own mix.

YIELD: 6 SERVINGS

3 russet potatoes

1 tbsp (15 ml) canola oil

2 tsp (10 g) seasoned salt

1. HEY KIDS, PLEASE GET US STARTED! →

Rinse and scrub the potatoes, and decide whether or not you'd like to peel them. Bits of potato skin on the fries can be extra yummy, but you can ask your adult helper to peel them if you prefer.

The potatoes need to be cut into matchstick shapes, which will require a large chef's knife. Ask your adult helper for assistance with this step.

Place the potato sticks in a large zip top plastic bag. Measure and pour in the canola oil and seasoned salt. Seal the top of the bag, and gently shake and toss the potatoes until they are all evenly coated in oil and seasoning.

Line a large baking sheet with parchment paper. Spread the potatoes on the sheet in an even single layer. If the potatoes are too crowded, use a second baking sheet to spread them out. If they are touching each other too much, they will steam instead of crisp up.

2. PARENTS, ← IT'S YOUR TURN!

Preheat the oven to 450°F (230°C, or gas mark 8). Help your kid chef to cut the potatoes into matchstick slices.

3. TEAMWORK GETS IT DONE!

Bake the potatoes for 40 to 45 minutes, tossing and flipping the fries halfway through the baking time so they crisp up evenly. If you used 2 pans, rotate which pan is on top halfway through baking.

Serve with ketchup or your favorite sauce for dipping.

GIANT GARLIC PARMESAN CHICKEN WINGS

Okay, these are actually chicken drummies, but we have a great excuse. Chicken wings are a family favorite appetizer at restaurants, but making them at home means such a tiny amount of meat for dinner. We giant-size our wings by making our favorite dish using chicken legs instead so there'd be more chicken for your effort! You're going to love how crispy the skin gets!

PLAY WITH IT! You can try brushing the chicken with your favorite barbecue sauce buffalo sauce or other condiment to switch the overall flavor of the "wings."

YIELD: 4 SERVINGS

1 (2-lb [896-g]) package of chicken drumsticks

1 tbsp (15 ml) olive oil

1 tsp seasoned salt

1 tsp garlic salt

¼ tsp cayenne pepper

3 tbsp (34 g) grated Parmesan cheese

1. HEY KIDS, PLEASE GET US STARTED!

Line a large baking sheet with tinfoil, and place all the chicken legs on the pan in a single layer. Make sure to not overcrowd the pan.

Brush olive oil over the tops of each leg with a pastry brush or the back of a spoon.

Measure and mix the seasoned salt, garlic salt and cayenne pepper in a small bowl. Sprinkle it evenly over both sides of each chicken leg.

2. PARENTS, IT'S YOUR TURN!

Preheat the oven to 450°F (230°C, or gas mark 8).

3. TEAMWORK GETS IT DONE!

Roast the chicken legs for 40 minutes, or until the skin is golden brown and crispy. Turn the chicken legs halfway through baking so they brown on all sides.

Immediately sprinkle the Parmesan cheese over the chicken, and let them rest for 5 minutes before serving.

You've Got Skills

MAKING THE PERFECT POT OF RICE

Rice is a delicious and simple side dish to serve with many family dinners. You only need to follow a few important rules to have your rice turn out perfectly every time.

1. Use a sturdy, heavy-bottomed pot with a lid.

2. Watch your heat. If it's too high your rice will stick.

3. Slightly vent your lid to let a little steam escape so the pot doesn't bubble over.

4. Always use a ratio of 2 to 1: 2 cups (473 ml) of water to 1 cup (211 g) of rice. If you want more rice, remember to increase the water.

Use the recipe for rice with lime and herbs to practice your awesome rice-making skills!

CILANTRO LIME RICE

Plain rice is a great choice if your dinner has a sauce that will run over it. If you want to enjoy the rice on its own, you can flavor it with a bit of butter or make this yummy Mexican-inspired rice dish!

YIELD: 4 SERVINGS

1 cup (211 g) jasmine rice or other white rice

2 cups (473 ml) water

Pinch of salt

1 lime

½ cup (20 g) fresh cilantro

Salt & pepper

1. HEY KIDS, PLEASE GET US STARTED!

Measure your rice and place it in a heavy-bottomed pot. Measure the water, and add it to the pot with a pinch of salt. Give the rice a gentle stir to combine it with the water.

2. PARENTS, IT'S YOUR TURN!

Turn a burner on the stove to medium-high.

3. TEAMWORK GETS IT DONE!

Bring the water with the rice to a gentle boil. You'll know it's ready when the water is bubbling up quickly with nice big bubbles. Give the rice a gentle stir to make sure nothing is sticking to the bottom. Then, immediately reduce the heat to low and place the lid over the pot. It's okay to slightly vent the lid to prevent the starchy water from boiling over onto your stove top.

As the rice continues to cook it will begin to soak up all the water in the pot. It will be harder for you to see any more liquid at the bottom of the pan, but the rice will continue to steam. Cook for 12 to 15 minutes, or until all the liquid has been absorbed by the rice. Then fluff the rice with a fork before you serve it.

If there is still water in the pot, you will need to cook it a few minutes more. If the rice has stuck to the bottom by the time you check on it, you can have your adult helper add a tablespoon or two (15 to 30 ml) of water to the hot pan, and then immediately stir and scrape the bottom to lift up the stuck rice.

Cut the lime in half, squeeze the juices into the rice, and stir. Chop the cilantro, and stir it into the rice. Season to taste with a pinch of salt and pepper.

PINEAPPLE CASHEW FRIED RICE

Next time you make rice, make a double batch so you can save some plain white rice for this fried rice the next night. When you know exactly what you put in it, all those hidden veggies are a lot less scary.

PLAY WITH IT! This dish is not too spicy at all but the red pepper flakes give it a little kick. You can add more or even a drizzle of Sriracha sauce if you like it hot. Leftover rotisserie chicken or cooked pork tenderloin are great additions, too.

YIELD: 4 TO 6 SERVINGS

1 small onion

1 red bell pepper

2 eggs

2 tsp (6 g) jarred minced garlic

½ tsp dried ginger

½ tsp red pepper flakes

3 tbsp (45 ml) vegetable oil

1 cup (120 g) pineapple chunks (fresh or canned)

½ cup (115 g) mixed frozen vegetables (corn, peas, carrots, green beans)

4 cups (644 g) leftover white rice or 1 quart (749 g) of plain white rice from your local Chinese food restaurant

⅓ cup (79 ml) soy sauce

½ cup (56 g) cashews

1. HEY KIDS, PLEASE GET US STARTED! ➤➤➤

Have your helper cut the onion into 4 quarters. Then have your helper open and remove the red pepper seeds so you can chop the onion and pepper up into little pieces in a manual food processor.

Crack the eggs into a small bowl, and use a fork to beat them until they are light yellow.

Measure the garlic, ginger and red pepper flakes, and put them in a small bowl near the stove.

2. PARENTS, ←— IT'S YOUR TURN!

Optional: Cut the pineapple chunks into smaller pieces if you prefer.

In a large skillet over medium-high heat, add the vegetable oil.

3. TEAMWORK GETS IT DONE!

Add the eggs to the oil, and stir them with a long-handled cooking spoon. When they are completely scrambled, add the garlic and seasonings mixture, the chopped veggies and the pineapple chunks to the pan.

Stir the veggies and sauté them until the onions are translucent, about 5 minutes. Measure and add the mixed frozen veggies to the pan, and cook for another minute.

Add the white rice to the pan, and use your spoon to break up the large chunks.

Measure and pour the soy sauce into the pan, and stir everything up to coat.

Measure and add the cashew pieces, and stir them into the rice. Continue to sauté the rice and veggies until the frozen veggies are heated through and the rice is piping hot.

POTSTICKER STIR-FRY

Our family fights over the potstickers every time we do take-out. We tried making them from scratch, but it took too long to be worth it. Instead, we took all the flavors of our favorite appetizer and turned them into a pasta stir-fry. Using rice noodles means you can cook them right in the same pot!

PLAY WITH IT! The red pepper flakes and cayenne here make for a very spicy dish. Be sure to leave them out for a milder pasta. You could add more peppers, broccoli florets or pea pods at the sauté stage for more veggies. Ginger or some sesame seeds would be great additions.

YIELD: 4 TO 6 SERVINGS

1 (16-oz [454-g]) package of rice noodles

½ red bell pepper

3 green onions

½ cup (118 ml) soy sauce

2 tbsp (30 ml) rice wine vinegar

1 tsp toasted sesame oil

1 tbsp (15 g) ketchup

2 tsp (10 g) mustard

1 tbsp (15 ml) Worcestershire sauce

1 tbsp (14 g) packed brown sugar

¼ tsp red pepper flakes

¼ tsp cayenne pepper

1 tbsp (15 ml) canola oil

1 lb (454 g) ground pork

2 tsp (6 g) jarred minced garlic

1 tsp pepper

3–4 cups (710–946 ml) chicken stock

1. HEY KIDS, PLEASE GET US STARTED! ➤

Fill a large mixing bowl with hot tap water. Soak the rice noodles while you prepare the rest of the dish.

Have your helper open and remove the seeds from the red pepper and cut it into chunks so you can chop it up into small pieces with a manual food processor. Put the chopped peppers in a small bowl near the stove.

Trim the tips off each end of the green onions, and throw the tips away. Then cut the onions in half, right where they turn from green to white. Chop all the greens together in the manual food processor, and then place them in a small bowl on your dining table. Then chop all the white parts together, and place those in the same bowl as the red peppers.

In a measuring cup, measure and add the soy sauce, rice wine vinegar and sesame oil. Use a fork to whisk it all together. Place the bowl near the stove.

Measure the ketchup, mustard, Worcestershire sauce, brown sugar, red pepper flakes and cayenne pepper into a separate small bowl. Set it aside near the stove.

2. PARENTS, IT'S YOUR TURN!

Place a large skillet over medium-high heat. Add the canola oil and ground pork.

3. TEAMWORK GETS IT DONE!

Brown the ground pork, chopping it up into small pieces with the back of a spoon, until it is no longer pink, about 7 to 10 minutes. If there is an excess of liquid in the pan, have your adult helper drain it off and return the pan to the stove.

Measure and add the garlic and black pepper to the skillet. Add the red peppers and white onion pieces. Sauté for 2 to 3 minutes until fragrant.

Scrape the bowl filled with the ketchup and seasonings mixture into the skillet. Stir it with a spoon, and cook for 2 to 3 minutes.

Pour in the soy sauce mixture, then measure and pour the 3 cups (710 ml) of chicken stock into the skillet. Give it a stir.

Drain the rice noodles from their soaking liquid. When the mixture in the skillet comes to a bubble, add the noodles to the pan.

Gently stir the noodles and nestle them into the liquid. Cover the skillet, and turn the heat down to medium-low. Cook the noodles for 15 to 20 minutes until tender. Add up to 1 more cup (237 ml) of chicken stock in ¼ cup (59 ml) batches if the noodles look like they are absorbing too much liquid and the mixture is getting dry. The dish should be nice and saucy with tender soft noodles.

Serve topped with fresh green onions.

CASHEW CHICKEN

Cashew chicken is yummy on its own, but it goes really well with either white rice or rice noodles. If you like things a little saucier, you can always add a little more chicken broth to thin it out.

PLAY WITH IT! This dish isn't at all spicy. If you like things hot, try adding some red pepper flakes to the sauce. You could also change the bell pepper to a different veggie such as broccoli or pea pods.

YIELD: 4 TO 6 SERVINGS

1 green bell pepper

⅓ cup (79 ml) soy sauce

1 tbsp (15 ml) hoisin sauce

1 tbsp (15 ml) rice vinegar

1 tbsp (14 g) packed brown sugar

½ tsp toasted sesame oil

1 tsp dried ginger

¼ cup (59 ml) chicken broth

2 tbsp (19 g) cornstarch

3 green onions

1 lb (454 g) boneless, skinless chicken tenderloins

3 tbsp (45 ml) vegetable oil

2 tsp (6 g) jarred minced garlic

1 cup (111 g) cashew pieces

1 batch of plain rice, for serving (optional)

1. HEY KIDS, PLEASE GET US STARTED!

Have your helper open and remove the seeds from the green pepper so you can chop it up into little pieces with a manual food processor.

Measure the soy sauce, hoisin sauce, rice vinegar, brown sugar, sesame oil and ginger, and stir them together in a small bowl or measuring cup. Set the bowl next to the stove.

Measure the chicken broth in a measuring cup, and add the cornstarch to it. Whisk the mixture with a fork until it is smooth, and then set it aside near the stove.

2. PARENTS, IT'S YOUR TURN!

Trim the ends from the green onions, and then chop them up. Set them aside in a small bowl.

Cut the chicken tenderloins into bite-size chunks, about 1-inch (2.5-cm) pieces.

In a large skillet, add the vegetable oil over medium-high heat.

3. TEAMWORK GETS IT DONE!

Add the chicken to the skillet and sauté until it is golden brown on all sides, 5 to 7 minutes. Add the bell pepper, then measure and add the garlic. Continue to sauté until the pieces are softened. Pour in the soy sauce mixture, and stir the skillet to coat the chicken.

Add the chicken broth and cornstarch mix to the pan, and stir to combine. Measure and stir in the cashew pieces. The sauce will become thick and bubbly; you can add a tablespoon (15 ml) of water to thin it out if it gets too thick.

Sprinkle the fresh green onions over the top, and serve with white rice if you like.

GENERAL TSO'S CHICKEN

When we order Chinese take-out, General Tso's chicken is always a favorite. It's nice and spicy, but it's even better when you can control just how spicy to make it. Sometimes homemade Chinese recipes require exotic ingredients to get the flavor right. This recipe includes items you should easily be able to find at your grocery store, but you may have to peek in the Chinese food aisle next to the soy sauces.

PLAY WITH IT! You can make this more or less spicy by changing how much red pepper flakes and garlic you put in. You can also change the veggies from broccoli to green bell peppers, pea pods, onions, asparagus or even canned baby corn if you can find it!

YIELD: 4 TO 6 SERVINGS

1 lb (454 g) boneless, skinless chicken thighs or breasts

¼ cup (38 g) cornstarch

Pinch of salt & pepper

½ cup (118 ml) tamari or soy sauce

⅓ cup (79 ml) water

3 tbsp (41 g) packed brown sugar

3 tbsp (44 ml) hoisin sauce

1 tsp toasted sesame oil

2 tbsp (30 ml) white vinegar

3 tbsp (46 g) ketchup

3 tsp (10 g) jarred minced garlic

½ tsp dried ginger

1 tsp dried red pepper flakes

3 tbsp (45 ml) vegetable oil

Chopped green onions, for garnish (optional)

1½ cups (344 g) fresh broccoli florets

1. HEY KIDS, PLEASE GET US STARTED!

Cut the chicken into bite-size chunks using a butter knife.

Measure the cornstarch and put it in a zip top baggie or large mixing bowl. Add the salt and pepper, and stir with a fork to combine. Add the chicken pieces to the cornstarch. Either close the baggie and gently toss to coat the chicken, or use a spoon to gently toss the chicken in the bowl.

Measure the tamari, water, brown sugar, hoisin, sesame oil, vinegar, ketchup, garlic, ginger and red pepper flakes. Combine them in a small mixing bowl. Set the bowl next to the stove.

2. PARENTS, IT'S YOUR TURN!

Place a large skillet over medium-high heat. Add the vegetable oil.

Trim the green onions and chop them. Put them in a bowl, and place them on the table for serving.

3. TEAMWORK GETS IT DONE!

When the vegetable oil begins to shimmer, the adult should add the chicken in small batches and brown on all sides, about 5 to 7 minutes. Using a slotted spoon, remove the cooked chicken to a plate while you finish the rest of the batch. If you overcrowd the pan, the chicken will not develop a golden crust.

Once the chicken has all been browned, pour the sauce into the pan and stir. When the sauce starts to bubble, add the chicken back to the pan. Add the broccoli florets, and stir to coat them in the sauce. Simmer until the chicken is completely cooked and the broccoli has heated through, about 5 to 7 minutes.

FEARLESS FOODIES ♥

Once you've mastered a few kitchen dishes, what keeps your menu from turning into an endless repeat? Learning to be more adventurous with the flavors you put on your plate!

It's very common for kids to tend to stick to a few food groups that are safe and comfortable. Jumping in feetfirst with something wild and crazy can be intimidating. We've found that a much better way is to gently dip our toes in the water by mixing familiar "safe" foods with an adventurous new spice or flavor, such as the Mustard Roasted Potatoes (page 186) or a whole new cooking method like the Roasted Spicy Broccoli (page 180), to ease in to more complicated recipes down the road.

The perfect place to play with these new combinations is in simple snacks like the Homemade Buttermilk Ranch Dressing veggie tray (page 188) and side dishes such as the Lime Corn Salad (page 184). When it's not the center of your whole meal, there's less chance you'll worry you've wasted an entire breakfast or dinner on a failed experiment. And who knows, maybe that little side dish will end up being your favorite part of the whole meal!

And kids, guess what the very best part of this chapter is?! You've learned so much now that these dishes can be 100 percent made by YOU! Mix together a few of the dishes from this section and you'll be able to make an entire meal for your family all by yourself. Look how far you've come!

You've Got Skills

HOW TO USE AN OVEN

The most important appliance for cooking dinner just happens to be the one that most parents get very nervous about letting kids explore. Ovens can bake, roast or broil just about anything, but they are also the leading cause of burns for chefs.

The goal of this book is to help build your confidence in the kitchen, but make sure you have the safety knowledge you need so you don't get hurt. With smart precautions, you can learn to stay safe from harm and learn to finish off a dinner all by yourself.

Just remember these important tips:

1. Always wear your oven mitts when putting anything in or taking anything out of the oven. The door and racks get super hot, so watch your hands.

2. Stand back from the door when you open the oven because a hot blast of air usually escapes. Lean back for a few seconds before peeking inside.

3. Every time you open the oven door, the temperature inside changes as the heat escapes. If you just need to peek at the food, try to use the light and look through the window of the door rather than opening it up to check.

Now let's try making a batch of the delicious garlicky knots on the next page to test your oven skills.

GARLIC KNOTS

When we order dinner delivery from our favorite pizza place, we can't resist adding on a side of their buttery garlic knots. They usually disappear faster than the pizza itself. Making them at home means we can bake a bigger batch, and tying the dough into knots is so much fun! These easy rolls go well with almost any dinner in this book, but we love them most with a batch of homemade soup.

PLAY WITH IT!: Garlic knots are a classic, but how about dressing them up with a new set of seasonings to make them extra special? You can try any of the seasoning blends from the popcorn blends on page 192 or mix your own. A sprinkle of cinnamon and sugar makes them sweet, but with a dash of rosemary and roasted pepper flakes you have an awesome roll to dip in the tomato soup on page 58. What extra-special pairings can you come up with?

YIELD: 16 KNOTS

1 (14-oz [391-g]) container refrigerated pizza dough OR 1 ball of pizza dough (page 142)

3 tbsp (43 g) butter

1 tsp garlic salt

½ tsp parsley

1. HEY KIDS, YOU CAN DO THIS ALL BY YOURSELF!

Preheat the oven to 400°F (200°C, or gas mark 6). Ask your adult helper to show you where the buttons are on your oven and to give you an introduction to the knobs and what they do. Be sure to pay attention to which knob controls which burner so you can use that information another time.

Get out a baking sheet and place it on the counter.

Open up the container of dough, and roll it out flat on a cutting board. Use a butter knife (or a pizza wheel if your adult helper says it is okay) to cut the dough into 8 long strips. Then cut each long strip in half to make a total of 16 pieces.

Take each strip of dough and twist it lengthwise, then swirl it into a roll shape. Place each twisted roll on your baking sheet, and repeat the steps with the remaining strips.

Measure the butter and melt it in a microwave-safe container for 30 seconds. Brush it on top of your knots of dough with a pastry brush or the back of a spoon.

Measure the garlic salt and parsley, and mix them together in a small bowl. Sprinkle them over the top of the knots.

Now is the time to put the knots inside the oven. To protect yourself from burns, we recommend wearing oven mitts on both of your hands the entire time you are placing the pan in the oven.

Open the oven door while standing back with your face away from the hot air that will be released. Give the oven 5 to 10 seconds to release the initial hot blast of air before you try to put the pan inside.

Holding the pan firmly, with both hands covered in mitts, carefully place the baking sheet on the center rack. Step back and carefully close the door.

Be careful to never touch the inside of the door or the racks of the oven.

Bake the knots for 8 to 10 minutes, or until golden brown. When you peek to check on them, always keep your face away from the hot blast of air when the door opens. It's even better if your oven has a light for you to turn on and check through the window.

While wearing both of your oven mitts for safety, carefully remove the knots from the oven. Place the baking sheet on the stove top. Never put a hot pan from the oven onto your kitchen counter or you could possibly melt the counter! Use a spatula to transfer the knots to a serving plate.

CREAMY FETA & WATERMELON SALAD

Why do you think people like nuts in their cookies or chocolate covered pretzels? Because salty + sweet is one of the best flavor combinations out there! So how can we use this to our advantage when we're making something healthy for our dinner?

If you think you don't like salad, then you just might love this challenge. Sweet juicy watermelon is the center of the dish rather than the standard salad lettuce. Mix it up with a few savory things, and taste how those two flavors make each other even better. If making your own salad dressing sounds too challenging right now, feel free to substitute a store-bought one instead! The point of this challenge is to try the flavor combination, so do what works best for you.

PLAY WITH IT! Watermelon isn't the only fruit that works well as a salad. Experiment with cantaloupe, pineapple, plums, apples or grapes mixed with your favorite salty things such as nuts, different cheeses or even bits of ham.

YIELD: 4 TO 6 SERVINGS

HOMEMADE FETA DRESSING
5 oz (142 g) crumbled feta

⅓ cup (79 ml) buttermilk

¾ cup (177 ml) sour cream

2 tbsp (30 ml) olive oil

2 tbsp (30 ml) white wine vinegar

2 tsp (7 g) jarred minced garlic

1 green onion, chopped

1 tsp dill

1 tsp oregano

Sprinkle of salt & pepper

SALAD
Fresh watermelon

Fresh basil leaves

Salted sunflower seeds

Fresh tomatoes

1. HEY KIDS, YOU CAN DO THIS ALL BY YOURSELF! ➤➔

Measure the feta, buttermilk, sour cream, olive oil, white wine vinegar, garlic, green onion, dill, oregano, salt and pepper. Whisk them together in a bowl. If you're using a store-bought dressing instead, place it at your table with a spoon.

Cut the fresh watermelon into large bite-size chunks with a butter knife, or use a chef's knife with parent approval. Place them in a serving bowl.

You can leave the basil leaves whole or tear them with your fingers into smaller pieces. Sprinkle them over the watermelon.

Sprinkle the salted sunflower seeds over the watermelon. Slice the fresh cherry tomatoes into halves, and sprinkle them into the salad.

You can assemble the salad as directed and serve with the dressing, or you can serve each ingredient in its own small bowl and let each diner at the table assemble their own salad as they prefer.

BALSAMIC VINAIGRETTE STRAWBERRY SALAD

"Eat the rainbow!" You've probably heard this colorful advice about making healthy choices. The more colors on your plate, the more healthful your meal can be. Many kids would rather skip the colorful veggies and wish they could simply eat fruit instead. This challenge helps make vegetables a little less scary by pairing them up with some of our favorite fruits.

PLAY WITH IT! Strawberries and baby spinach are delicious together, but you can enjoy a fruity salad any time of year. Try mixing things up with one of these combinations instead: A) apples + carrots; B) pineapple + peppers; C) grapes + broccoli; D) oranges + pea pods.

YIELD: 4 TO 6 SERVINGS

BALSAMIC VINAIGRETTE SALAD DRESSING

3 tbsp (45 ml) balsamic vinegar

1 tbsp (16 g) Dijon mustard

1 tsp jarred minced garlic

½ cup (118 ml) olive oil

Sprinkle of salt & pepper

STRAWBERRY SALAD

Balsamic vinegar salad dressing (store-bought or homemade recipe above)

1 (6-oz [170-g]) bag baby spinach salad mix

2 cups (303 g) fresh strawberries

½ cup (56 g) pistachios

5 oz (142 g) crumbled feta or goat cheese (optional)

1. HEY KIDS, YOU CAN DO THIS ALL BY YOURSELF! ➤➤➤

If you are making the homemade salad dressing, simply measure and add the vinegar, mustard, garlic, olive oil, salt and pepper to a jar with a lid. Close it tightly, and shake it vigorously over your sink in case it leaks.

Wash and dry the baby spinach salad in a salad spinner. Place it in a large serving bowl.

Wash and dry the strawberries. Use a butter knife, or a paring knife with parent approval, to cut off the leafy tops and then cut them into smaller pieces. Add them to the salad bowl.

Sprinkle fresh pistachios over the salad. Sprinkle the crumbled cheese over the bowl, if you like.

Toss the salad together with 2 large spoons. Serve with the salad dressing on the side.

ROASTED SPICY BROCCOLI

Hey, lean in close for a second. I have a secret to tell you . . . I really, really didn't like broccoli when I was a kid. My mom always steamed it and served it plain with salt and pepper. It wasn't until I was all grown up and discovered broccoli tasted different when you cooked it in different ways that I finally learned to love it. Now it is one of my favorite vegetables!

Sometimes we think we don't like something, but the truth is we may just not like it prepared that one way. Next time you find you don't like a vegetable, try to remember that you might like it raw or roasted or steamed better. Can you think of one you'd like to experiment on right now? Here's the recipe that made me fall in love with broccoli. Maybe it will work for you, too.

PLAY WITH IT! This method works well with cauliflower, carrots, green beans, and so many more vegetables. Just mix up the veggie and use your favorite seasoning blend.

YIELD: 4 SERVINGS

1 head of fresh broccoli

2 tsp (10 ml) olive oil

½ tsp crushed red pepper flakes

Sprinkle of salt & pepper

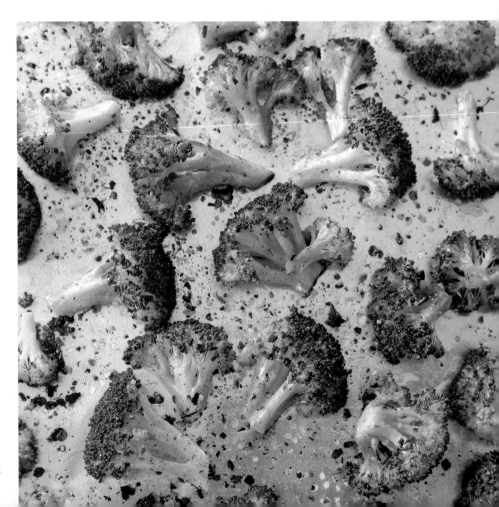

1. HEY KIDS, YOU CAN DO THIS ALL BY YOURSELF! ➤━━➤

Rinse the broccoli under cold water, and gently shake it off in the sink. Dry it with a clean kitchen towel.

Cut the broccoli florets off of the head with a butter knife, or use a chef's knife with parent approval. Preheat the oven to 450°F (230°C, or gas mark 8).

Line a cookie sheet with some tinfoil. Place the broccoli florets on the cookie sheet, and drizzle the olive oil over the top. Use your hands to toss the veggies and coat them in the oil. Wash and dry your hands.

Measure and sprinkle the red pepper flakes, salt and pepper over the broccoli. Roast for 15 minutes. When it's ready, the broccoli will be slightly charred and crispy.

BETTER THAN BOXED MAC & CHEESE

Kids love macaroni and cheese, but the question always remains: to blue box or not to blue box? Once you taste this homemade version, you will never look back. It's easy and totally creamy, and it has just the right amount of sauce. Not too soupy, thank you! The best part? You can change the shape of the noodle to whatever you enjoy the most.

PLAY WITH IT! You can change the flavor by swapping out different cheese blends. Colby Jack, cheddar, Swiss, Parmesan—use what you love. How about making it a Mexi-Mac and stir in some taco seasoned cheddar and a can of Ro-Tel diced tomatoes and peppers?

YIELD: 6 TO 8 SERVINGS

1 lb (454 g) pasta shells

4 oz (113 g) meltable prepared cheese, such as Velveeta

2 tbsp (29 g) butter

1 cup (237 ml) milk

1 cup (121 g) shredded cheddar cheese blend

¼ tsp seasoned salt

Sprinkle of black pepper

1. HEY KIDS, YOU CAN DO THIS ALL BY YOURSELF! ➤——→

Set a big pot of salted water over high heat. Once the water is boiling, add the pasta shells and stir. Be sure to cook them for the lowest time listed on the package. Drain the pasta in a colander in the sink, asking an adult helper for help moving the heavy pot if you need to. Return the empty pot to the stove.

While the pasta cooks, measure and cut the meltable cheese into large chunks. Set it aside.

Once the pasta has been drained, measure and add the butter to the pot over medium-low heat. Once it's melted, measure and pour in the milk, cheddar cheese blend, meltable cheese, seasoned salt and a pinch of black pepper. Gently whisk it until the cheeses are both melted and the sauce is smooth.

Return the drained pasta to the pot, and stir it up to combine with the sauce. Serve immediately.

LIME CORN SALAD

When we're talking about our food preferences, sometimes it is easier to focus on the things we don't like instead of the things that we do. However, I'm sure if you sat down and listed all the foods that you love, you'd have a pretty long list. Did you ever think about trying a new food matched with something you know you already love? Every summer we visit the farmers' market and find new veggies to try. When my kids get suspicious about a new one, we toss it in with a salad made of fresh sweet corn that we know they love. The yummy corn can help hide the scarier new veggies.

PLAY WITH IT! You can add almost any summer vegetable to this mix! Green peppers, broccoli, tomatoes, spinach or green beans would all be delicious.

YIELD: 6 TO 8 SERVINGS

3 cobs of fresh corn, boiled and corn cut from the cobs or 1 (12-oz [340-g]) package of thawed frozen corn

½ cup (80 g) cherry tomatoes

½ cup (90 g) radishes

1 jalapeño pepper

1 lime

2 tbsp (30 ml) olive oil

Salt & pepper

1. HEY KIDS, YOU CAN DO THIS ALL BY YOURSELF! ➤ ⟶

Place the prepared corn in a large mixing bowl. Cut the cherry tomatoes in half with a butter knife, or a chef's knife with parent approval, and add them to the bowl. Carefully cut the radishes into slices if you can. Otherwise, chunks will work too.

Carefully cut off the top of the jalapeño (where the stem is). Then cut the pepper down the middle, lengthwise. Use a spoon to scoop out the seeds into the garbage can. Try not to touch the seeds or ribs with your hands. Chop the jalapeño into small pieces. Wash your hands immediately after to rinse away the spicy oils from the pepper.

Wash and cut the lime in half and squeeze the juice into the corn bowl.

Measure and drizzle the olive oil into the corn bowl. Sprinkle a pinch of salt and pepper into the bowl.

Toss the veggies together to coat them in the olive oil and lime juices. This dish can be served at room temperature or cold.

MUSTARD-ROASTED POTATOES

Ketchup is usually a kid's favorite dip of choice, but have you ever looked closely at the condiment aisle of a grocery store? There are oodles of options for you to play with: smoky barbecue sauce, spicy hot sauce, fresh pesto, salty soy sauce, hot wasabi, savory steak sauce and vinegary mustard.

Even a single type of condiment comes in many flavors like Dijon mustard, spicy mustard, honey mustard and more. If you have avoided all mustard because you don't like the plain yellow variety, you're missing out!

PLAY WITH IT! Condiments aren't just for dipping, they can be used to add flavor to our food when we cook it, too. We love to make these Mustard Roasted Potatoes with whole-grain mustard, but any mustard you love would work equally well! Or skip the mustard when cooking and use the plain roasted potatoes as a way to taste test a few different condiments to see which one you like best.

YIELD: 4 TO 6 SERVINGS

2 lbs (907 g) baby red potatoes

1 large onion

3 tbsp (45 ml) olive oil

2 tbsp (31 g) whole-grain mustard

Sprinkle of salt & pepper

A second mustard for dipping—choose from honey mustard, Dijon or a spicy mustard of your choice (optional)

1. HEY KIDS, YOU CAN DO THIS ALL BY YOURSELF!

Preheat the oven to 425°F (220°C, or gas mark 7). Rinse and scrub the red potatoes until they are clean. Let them dry on a clean kitchen towel.

Place a large baking sheet on the counter.

Use a butter knife, or a chef's knife with parent approval, to cut the potatoes into halves or quarters. Each cut potato should be roughly the same size so they cook evenly. Place the potatoes on the baking sheet.

Cut the onion into large wedges and place them on the baking sheet.

Measure and drizzle the olive oil over the potatoes and onions, then add the mustard. Use your hands to toss all the onions and potatoes with the oil and mustard until everything is coated. Spread them out in a single layer.

Wash your hands. Then sprinkle salt and pepper over the top of the potato mixture. Bake for 50 minutes to 1 hour, but set a timer for every 20 minutes so you can toss them with a spatula. The bottoms will get nice and crispy and the onions will begin to char, watch that the potatoes don't burn.

HOMEMADE BUTTERMILK RANCH DRESSING

Hopefully the new condiment challenge introduced you to a new favorite or two. Once we have our favorites, trying new foods becomes a lot less scary if we can dip them in something we know we love. Try to take a field trip to the grocery store produce section and find one or two new vegetables you haven't tried yet. Using this fun experiment, one of my daughters discovered she loves radishes and the other sweet pea pods.

PLAY WITH IT! We love to dip our raw veggies in a homemade buttermilk ranch, but if you prefer another salad dressing or condiment, feel free to use your favorite one. Your veggie platter will reflect the season you are in. Find ones that are fresh and colorful.

YIELD: 10 TO 12 SERVINGS

½ cup (118 ml) buttermilk

½ cup (118 ml) sour cream

¼ cup (55 g) mayonnaise

2 tsp (7 g) jarred minced garlic

1 tsp salt

¼ tsp pepper

1 tsp dill

½ tsp dried parsley

¼ tsp onion powder

Juice from ½ lemon

¼ cup (12 g) chopped fresh chives

1. HEY KIDS, YOU CAN DO THIS ALL BY YOURSELF! ➤➔

Measure the buttermilk and pour it into a mixing bowl. Measure the sour cream and mayonnaise, and add them to the bowl. Whisk them together until smooth. Measure and add the garlic, salt, pepper, dill, parsley and onion powder to the dressing, and whisk them in until smooth.

Wash and cut a lemon in half, and squeeze the juice into the dressing. Use your fingers to catch the seeds so they don't fall in! Chop the fresh chives and stir them into the dressing. Set the dressing aside in the refrigerator.

Head to the grocery store or farmers' market with your adult helper for a treasure hunt for a new veggie or two. Ask them about which veggies were their favorites, but also about which ones they didn't like as a kid and how they discovered they do like them.

Wash and prepare the raw veggies for your dipping platter. Some things, such as radishes, are better when cut into very thin slices. Other things, such as broccoli, are better in larger chunks. Cut the veggies up as needed, and arrange them on a pretty plate. Serve alongside the dressing for dipping.

Flat-Leaf Parsley

Scallions / Green Onions

Bay Leaves

Cinnamon Sticks

Ground Cumin

Red Pepper Flakes

Black Peppercorns

You've Got Skills

IDENTIFYING HERBS AND SPICES

Herbs and spices can be found fresh from the produce section of the grocery store or your garden, or look for dried ones in the spice aisle of the grocery store. These ingredients are what give most of our food a pleasant flavor. How much or how little you use is all up to you. With any recipe you make you can adjust the amount of spices to match your tastes. It's part of what makes cooking your own food so fun!

There are too many for us to list here, but here are some of the most kid-friendly flavor boosters. Can you find them in your spice collection? Take a few minutes to look at them and sniff them. Which one smells the best?

Italian
You'll find these hiding in your favorite pizza, spaghetti and garlic bread.

PARSLEY: We love fresh, flat-leaf Italian parsley the best, but dried works, too. This is often used as a garnish to make your food look pretty, but it is also delicious.

BASIL: Fresh basil is the best choice whenever possible. Did you know it is really easy to grow at home in a pot? We love to make our own pesto with it.

OREGANO: Dried oregano is the easiest to use and keep. It gives a special flavor to many soups and sauces.

THYME: Dried thyme is the secret ingredient to many of our favorite foods. How many recipes in this book can you spot it listed?

Mexican
Without these, your salsa would just be tomato sauce and your tacos would be just plain chicken!

CILANTRO: Most people either love fresh cilantro or hate it. Which team are you on? We are definitely on Team Love. It's the key to homemade salsa.

CUMIN: Dried cumin smells like tacos in a jar. We use it for chilis and soups, too.

CHILI POWDER: There are many varieties of dried chili powder available. Most recipes in this book call for a regular mild, but you can swap it for a spicier variety if you like.

Asian
These tend to bring a little more kick to our dishes. If you want to add some heat, this is a great place to start.

CINNAMON: You are probably thinking of cinnamon rolls, but it can also be used in savory dishes, too!

RED PEPPER FLAKES: A simple sprinkle of these red pepper flakes will bring instant spice to your dishes. We love to use them for a little kick in our Asian foods, but they also work great in many Italian dishes, too!

GINGER: Fresh ginger can be found at the grocery store, but it has a much stronger flavor than dried. Ease in with the dried version until you're sure you love it.

PERFECT POPCORN, THREE WAYS

A great way to get familiar with the spices in your kitchen is to taste them. Why not host a popcorn tasting party with a big batch of popcorn seasoned a few different ways? Have everyone vote for their favorite. Here are three blends to get you going, but you could try any seasoning combo you like!

PLAY WITH IT!: Once you've experimented with the seasoning blends here, why not try to make your own? Here's a hint to get you started: Pay attention to the flavors described on menus when you go out to eat with your family. Read through the whole menu, even if you always order the same thing. Make a list of things you find new or interesting, and see if you can find the same spices and flavorings in your own pantry when you get back home.

YIELD: 6 TO 8 SERVINGS

ITALIAN POPCORN SEASONING MIX
1 tsp garlic salt

2 tsp (1 g) dried oregano

1 tsp dried basil

1 tsp red pepper flakes

¼ cup (45 g) grated Parmesan cheese

MEXICAN POPCORN SEASONING MIX
1 tsp cumin

1 tsp chili powder

½ tsp oregano

½ tsp garlic salt

Juice from 1 lime

ASIAN POPCORN SEASONING MIX
½ tsp cinnamon

½ tsp dried ginger

¼ tsp cumin

Sprinkle of red pepper flakes

PERFECT POPCORN
3 tbsp (45 ml) canola oil

½ cup (100 g) popcorn kernels

3 tbsp (43 g) butter (optional)

1. HEY KIDS, YOU CAN DO THIS ALL BY YOURSELF! ➤——→

Choose which seasoning blend you want to try on your popcorn. Measure and mix the matching ingredients in a small bowl, and set it aside while you make the popcorn.

Place a heavy-bottomed pot over medium-high heat.

Measure and add the canola oil to the pot along with 3 popcorn kernels. When they pop, you know the oil is hot enough for the rest of the popcorn. Carefully add the remaining kernels, but keep your hand away from the hot oil in the pot. It's best to wear an oven mitt so that the oil doesn't splash you. Gently swirl the pot so the kernels become covered in the oil.

Cover the pot loosely with a lid so that steam can escape. The popcorn is done popping when you can count to 8 without hearing a "pop."

Carefully lift the lid of the pot away, and keep your face away from the hot steam. Then, while wearing oven mitts, pour the hot popcorn into a large mixing bowl and toss it immediately with the seasoning blend of your choice.

Optional: Melt the butter in a microwave-safe container for 30 seconds, and drizzle it over the popcorn before you toss it with the seasoning blend.

GUACAMOLE FOR BEGINNERS

Sometimes it's not the flavor of a food that is unappealing, it's the texture. While we can improve the flavor by adding seasonings, we can improve the texture by preparing the food in a new way or adding other ingredients with texture that we do love.

The perfect example? I love crunchy corn, but mushy avocados are not my favorite. Put them together and the crunch of the corn helps me overlook the texture of the avocado. Then add in tortilla chips for dunking? Suddenly, we have snack heaven.

PLAY WITH IT! You can add more or less of any of the ingredients here that you like. You can't mess this one up. Love the corn but not the tomato? Go ahead and leave it out.

YIELD: 6 TO 8 SERVINGS

1 (11-oz [312-g]) can of Mexicorn (corn mixed with chopped red and green peppers)

1 large tomato

½ red onion

2 tsp (7 g) jarred minced garlic

1 lime

½ tsp salt

¼ tsp cumin

½ fresh jalapeño

3 whole avocados

½ cup (20 g) cilantro leaves

1. HEY KIDS, YOU CAN DO THIS ALL BY YOURSELF! ➤———→

Open the can of Mexicorn, and drain the liquid into the sink. Dump the corn into a large bowl.

Cut the tomato and onion into quarters. Chop them up into small pieces with a manual food processor, or use a chef's knife with parent approval. Add them to the mixing bowl with the corn.

Measure and add the garlic to the mixing bowl. Wash and cut the lime in half, and squeeze the juice into the bowl. Add the salt and ground cumin to the bowl, and stir everything up with a spatula.

Cut the top off of the jalapeño and then carefully cut it in half. Remove the ribs and seeds with a small spoon, and discard them. Chop half of the jalapeño, and add it to the mixing bowl of veggies. Wash your hands.

Cut the avocados in half—you won't be able to cut all the way through because of the pit inside. Just rotate your butter knife around it and then use your hands to twist the two halves apart. Use a spoon to remove the pit, and toss the pit out. Use a large spoon to scoop the avocado flesh out of the shell, and place it in the mixing bowl.

Chop the cilantro. Set it aside.

Gently stir the avocado with the other vegetables. Add the cilantro and stir again. Serve with tortilla chips for dunking.

Optional: You can bake store-bought chips on a baking sheet in the oven at 350°F (175°C, or gas mark 4) for 3 to 5 minutes to warm them up before serving. This makes everything taste like you're sitting at a real Mexican restaurant!

ZUCCHINI APPLE BREAD

Sometimes when we introduce a new food to our palette, it is easier to do it by focusing on the flavor and hiding the texture. Once you've learned to love the flavor, it is easier to accept the texture. Even as an adult, I'm working on appreciating the texture of bananas, but I enjoy them baked inside a quick bread. My girls struggle with the texture of zucchini, but love the flavor they give to this simple breakfast treat.

PLAY WITH IT! Other fruits and veggies that make for great quick breads include: carrots, bananas, sweet potato, pears, pumpkin, figs, cranberries and pineapple. You can even add nuts for a little crunch.

YIELD: 6 SERVINGS

1 tbsp (14 g) butter at room temperature

2 large eggs

½ cup (118 ml) vegetable oil

1 tsp vanilla extract

⅔ cup (128 g) granulated sugar

⅓ cup (73 g) packed brown sugar

1⅓ cups (133 g) all-purpose flour

1 tsp baking soda

½ tsp cinnamon

¼ tsp nutmeg

⅔ cup (227 g) shredded zucchini

½ cup (90 g) shredded apples

1. HEY KIDS, YOU CAN DO THIS ALL BY YOURSELF! ➤➤➤➤

Rub the softened butter all over the inside of an 8 x 4-inch (20 x 10-cm) loaf pan. Set aside.

Crack the eggs into a large mixing bowl. Watch for any bits of shell! Measure and add the vegetable oil and vanilla extract, and whisk it together until smooth and yellow.

Measure and add the granulated sugar and brown sugar to the bowl. Use a spatula to stir it together with the eggs until smooth. Measure and add the flour, baking soda, cinnamon and nutmeg to the bowl. Stir until the batter is wet with no dry patches of flour.

Carefully shred the zucchini and apples using a box grater or food processor. Keep your fingers away from the blades and just go slowly.

Preheat the oven to 350°F (175°C, or gas mark 4).

Stir the zucchini and apples into the batter. Spoon the batter into the prepared loaf pan. Bake for 50 minutes, or until a toothpick pricked in the center of the loaf comes out clean.

Don't Drop Your Spoon and Run!
MAKING MEALTIME SPECIAL

Just like cooking can't start until you have all your ingredients, preparing a meal doesn't end when the food is ready. In fact, that's just the beginning! The grand finale for all your hard work is finally getting to enjoy a lovely meal that you prepared with your family.

PLATE LIKE A PRO

Have you ever seen a cooking competition on television? The judges only get to taste test the food after it has been artfully presented on a dinner plate. They don't walk up to the soup pot in the kitchen and stick their spoon in for a taste. They wait for the food to come to them, ready to be enjoyed.

We eat with our eyes first. Food that looks pretty, colorful and fresh will make our tummies rumble long before our tongue gets its chance to taste it. You've gone to the effort of making the dinner. Go that last little step and learn to plate your food like a pro.

1. If you're dining family-style, place your food on a pretty platter or plate to bring to the table. Don't forget to put a serving spoon or fork on the platter so everyone can help themselves.

2. If you're serving up individual plates, don't pile too much food on all at once. If they are hungry, they can come back for a second serving. Leave some room between the edge of the food and the edge of the dish so the food doesn't look overwhelming.

3. Leave a space on the plate for your side dishes or a roll. A small serving of everything can go on the plate, just leave enough room for your whole menu.

4. Watch your splatters. Don't just slap the food onto the plate; transfer it from your pot to the dish carefully so that the plate remains clean where food isn't touching. If it gets too messy, you can wipe the rim of the dish with a dampened paper towel to clean it up.

5. Sprinkle on some color. Maybe it's a little fresh chopped parsley or green onions. A little sprinkle of something green makes most food look a lot prettier.

TEN WAYS TO COMPLIMENT THE CHEF (EVEN WHEN YOU DON'T LIKE THE FOOD)

You know how hard you've worked on this dish. Imagine what it might feel like if the first words out of everyone's mouth were: "I don't like this!" Here are some fantastic things you can learn to say at the dinner table to make whoever prepared the food feel loved and appreciated, even when you're not certain you like the food.

1. "Wow! You really worked hard on this meal. Thank you."
2. "That food looks so colorful. What a great job you've done planning this dinner!"
3. "Something smells so good. I can't wait to taste it!"
4. "I don't think I've ever tried this dish before. It will be interesting to taste it!"
5. "Is there a secret ingredient in here? I taste something special, and I can't tell what it is!"
6. "I've had a long day. Eating dinner with you is exactly what I needed tonight."
7. "What was the hardest part about making this dinner? I can tell you put in a lot of effort!"
8. "Did you try making this a different way than usual? I'd love to hear how it worked out for you!"
9. "Thank you for making me this dinner. Next time I'd love to try making it even spicier." (Or "with more chicken" or "with fewer peppers," etc.)
10. "Is this a new recipe? How did you decide to make this for our dinner tonight?"

TEN WAYS TO DESCRIBE YOUR DINNER THAT ANY CHEF WILL LOVE TO HEAR

1. Mouthwatering
2. Delectable
3. Mind-blowing
4. Amazing
5. Best Ever
6. Delicious
7. Tasty
8. Favorite
9. Total Keeper
10. Make Again

FUN DINNERTIME CONVERSATION GAMES TO PLAY WITH YOUR FAMILY

While everyone is enjoying their food, now is the time to connect as a family and find out how everyone is doing. If you need a little help getting the conversation started, here are some fun games to play that won't disrupt your meal.

HIGH — LOW — THANKFUL

Take turns in rounds and have everyone answer the following questions:

1. What was the best part of your day?
2. What was the worst part of your day?
3. What are you thankful for today?

WOULD YOU RATHER?

Take turns posing a "would you rather?" question and provide two options that are really tricky to choose between. Everyone gets to come up with a question, and everyone at the table has to take a turn to answer the question before the next person has a turn to ask a new question.

1. Would you rather jump out of an airplane or deep-sea dive in a shark tank?
2. Would you rather eat ice cream or chocolate cake every day for the rest of your life?
3. Would you rather go to the beach or camp in the mountains?
4. Would you rather work at the circus or run a zoo?

TRUE OR FALSE?

Each person takes a turn saying one fact they know is true and one that they know is false, and everyone else has to guess which is which. This can be facts about yourself or facts you've learned in school.

1. "I ate lunch with Billie today." OR "The math test I took was really tricky."
2. "I'm reading Harry Potter at school." OR "I had a dream about unicorns last night."
3. "There are beaches with pink sand." OR "Frogs are warm blooded."

ACKNOWLEDGMENTS

Thank you to the team at Page Street Publishing for helping me fulfill a dream of a lifetime. Without Will and Sarah and the rest of the crew, this book would have only existed in my kitchen.

Thank you to all the women who supported my career: Julie Finlay for teaching me to accept critique with an open mind, Maria Bailey for pushing me to create a product of my own, Carey Pace for encouraging me to practice food photography, and countless women in the blogging community who helped me to believe my voice adds value, and taught me how to get it heard. Thanks to a man smart enough to surround himself with brilliant women, Johnathan Crawford, who taught me how to hustle.

Thank you to my dear friend Moira and her sweet mother "Santa Ester" who gave me some of my first grown-up cooking lessons and encouraged me to try new foods with an open mind.

Thank you to the real-world moms of The Peanut Gallery who gave me crucial feedback and peeks into their own family kitchens as I developed the recipes for this book.

Thank you to Nya and Lola Harrington for being my virtual test kids. I imagined what we would try to share with you as I wrote each recipe. Thank you for letting me borrow your amazing mom, Zina Harrington. Without her cheerleading sessions, brainstorming brilliance and constant daily encouragement, I could not have written this book.

Thank you to Michelle Malek who answered countless cooking questions and lead the way with kid-friendly recipe ideas back when our peanuts were tiny. Few things make me happier than being able to taste test these dishes with you right in my kitchen.

Thank you to my sister Molly Tumanic for encouraging me to break a few rules in the kitchen. You helped me bring the playful attitude to these recipes I hope the kids will love.

Thanks to Mom and Dad for cleaning up my messes, running my errands and cheering me on so I could keep my focus and finish this special project. The fond memories from our family table are at the core of everything here.

Most of all, thank you to my family who put up with more dirty dishes and photo prop chaos than anyone could possibly imagine. Sophie and Charlotte, you two are my very best cheerleaders and taste testers. You lifted me up when I was filled with doubt, this book would be nothing without you. Thank you for your patience and love as I chased this dream. And to the most patient of husbands, Tim, thank you for tolerating the chaos and talking me down from the ledge time and time again. It's not easy being married to a creative woman, but you make me believe you wouldn't have it any other way. When you three hold this book, you're holding a tangible piece of my love for you in your hands. Eating dinner with you is the best part of my day.

ABOUT THE AUTHOR

Tiffany Dahle is a self-taught family chef with over ten years of experience. Her daughters and husband put her through rigorous on-the-job training which included studies in "Picky Eating 101" and "Food Aversions in Adults: A Perspective." Cooking for her family is a lifelong pursuit made infinitely easier by the two young assistant chefs she has added to her team.

Tiffany is the founder of Peanut Blossom, an online community for busy moms who want real-world, family-tested, kid-friendly food. She provides ongoing creative inspiration, helping parents celebrate the everyday moments that become cherished childhood memories. You can find her work on Country Living, Parents, Woman's Day, BuzzFeed and Melissa & Doug's Play Time Press.

INDEX